The Home Equity Kit

The Home Equity Kit

ANDREW JAMES McLEAN

WILEY

JOHN WILEY & SONS

New York • Chichester • Brisbane • Toronto • Singapore

Library of Congress Cataloging-in-Publication Data

McLean, Andrew James.
The home equity kit / by Andrew James McLean.
    p. cm.
  Bibliography: p.
  Includes index.
  ISBN 0-471-50641-9.—ISBN 0-471-50642-7 (pbk.)
  1. Real estate investment. 2. Retirement income. I. Title.
HD 1382.5.M317   1989
332.63'24—dc19   89–5515
                                          CIP

This book is dedicated to Dr. Jerry Buss, owner of the Great Western Forum and the renowned Los Angeles Lakers. Also, a special thanks to Mike Hamilton for giving life to a great idea.

PREFACE

With its value fattened by inflation and years of seemingly endless mortgage payments, the family residence can now be a practical source of retirement income. But if you don't already own property how do you go about acquiring an adequate retirement estate? And for those of you who already own a home or other investment realty, how do you decide what is the best way to convert all this accumulated equity into income?

You have several alternatives, and the advantages of each will be carefully analyzed in Part Four. Factoring in your age, your financial condition, and your family's specific wants and needs, you should find it easier to select the best method suited to "retire on the house."

The disposition of the home you're living in deserves special attention. If you decide to sell it, should you accept all cash or carry an interest-bearing note? You might even decide to rent the home. What about renting or buying a replacement home? If you buy, is it better to pay all cash or finance the replacement home? You could also stay in your present home and take out a variety of special types of loans that produce tax-free income.

For those of you just getting started in real estate, this book provides a wealth of ideas on how to acquire enough real estate to achieve a rich and laid-back retirement. The first three parts of this book offer you a complete do-it-yourself guide on how to profitably invest in residential property and build wealth for the future.

This book provides you with proven investment techniques not found anyplace else. It features the Buy-Option strategy, one that produces a return on investment that far exceeds conventional techniques, as well as several no-money-down strategies.

The Home Equity Kit is not just another "get rich quick" book on real estate. Instead, it offers sound advice about proven investment techniques while pointing out certain pitfalls to avoid. Specifically, it concentrates on investing in single-family homes and small multi-unit buildings.

Written in a conversational style and blended with my personal investing experiences, this book will serve as an excellent guide for both the lay person and professional. Whether you're entirely new to real estate investing, or already a homeowner or investor, you'll find a wide range of topics advising you on profitable investment opportunities.

Here is a sample of what this book offers you:

- It features an in-depth comparison of all the alternative ways to tap retirement income from the equity in your home.
- If you don't already own your home, it shows you how to buy one; then how to pyramid it into a multi-property estate on which you can retire.
- It shows you how to manage your holdings, without hassles.
- It shows you how to evaluate specific investment opportunities.
- It fully explains the key ingredients for profitable realty investing.
- It presents a special section on financing real estate, with emphasis on how to avoid paying too much for the wrong financing.
- It advises you on how to be tax wise and dollar smart, using the latest tax implications of real estate ownership.

Above all else, this book provides a flexible approach to comfortable long-term retirement, and a way to attain financial freedom through profitable realty investing. Best of luck to you and yours.

ANDREW J. MCLEAN

Naples, Florida
August 1989

CONTENTS

The Home Equity Kit

PART ONE
How You Can Retire on the House

1 INTRODUCTION

Introducing: a complete do-it-yourself guide to comfortable retirement in 15 to 20 years. And you can do it all in your spare time. *The Home Equity Kit* begins with a discussion of inflation and retirement planning, then takes you step-by-step through every phase of real estate investing. You'll be advised on how to get it together during various stages of a lifetime, then how to evaluate, negotiate, purchase, and profitably manage your holdings.

If you're a first-time investor, Part Two will show you how to get started. But even if you're a seasoned pro, you'll discover profitable ideas and techniques not found anyplace else. In particular, pay special attention to the Buy-Option technique. It offers the investor profit potential beyond any other form of investment.

Additionally, Part Four is a special section: How To Tap Retirement Income from Home Equity. This section is for those of you who wish to tap retirement income from realty holdings already acquired.

MAKING INFLATION WORK FOR YOU

Expecting wealth from bank savings is an impossible dream. The combined effects of inflation and income taxes erode any potential real growth in a common savings account. In fact, money left in an interest-bearing savings account actually loses its value.

If you were able to save $3000 annually, earning compound interest at 6 percent, after 20 years the accumulated sum would amount to $110,000. Quite a tidy sum, but if inflation averages 6 percent annually, in 20 years that $110,000 will only be worth about $37,000 in today's dollars. That's hardly adequate for a laid-back retirement. This is the danger of keeping your money in conservative fixed investments.

So how do you overcome this erosion, caused by inflation, of your hard-earned dollars? The answer lies in real estate. You need real estate, not only as a place to call home, but also as a hedge against the crippling effects of inflation and income taxes. On average, real estate has historically outperformed the rate of inflation. Furthermore, in most cases, investment in real estate offers you the ability to shelter ordinary wage income.

Investment in real estate not only offers you a proven method to develop financial security for you and your family, but also greater control than you have with other forms of investment. You know what it looks like. You can visit it. You can keep track of the neighborhood and tenants. And you don't need investment counselors' or stock brokers' advice—which may or may not be *sound* advice—to help you make your decisions.

Other forms of investment, such as commodities, stocks, and precious metals, are all vulnerable to drastic up-and-down price movement. Nor do they offer the investor any form of tax-shelter benefits.

On the other hand, real estate endures in historically stable markets. Its value will tend to fluctuate somewhat; but over the long term, virtually every well-located property endures these up-and-down swings and appreciates in value. Inflation accounts for most of this increase, but another contributing factor is real estate's unique characteristic of increasing demand. This is caused by an ever-growing population and the limited supply of land (they just aren't making any more of it).

Inflation and Appreciation

In simple terms, inflation is a loss in purchasing power of the dollar. To survive financially, you need an investment vehicle that outperforms the rate of inflation by a large margin.

If you make the mistake of keeping large amounts of money in savings, you actually lose money. If inflation is averaging 6 percent annually and you're earning 5 percent, that's a 1 percent loss. To make things worse, you have to pay income taxes on the 5 percent earnings. At a 28 percent tax rate, you're actually losing $2.40 on each $100 invested in savings.

Conversely, real estate has historically been very sensitive to the effects of inflation. So much so, that when the rate of inflation is averaging 6 percent, real estate values will usually appreciate 9 percent, on average, during the same time period. In addition, gains on real estate are not necessarily taxed; and in certain cases, income earned on real estate can actually shelter normal salary income.

There are other factors that help account for this appreciation of real estate. One has to do with what is called "replacement cost." Every time a plumber, carpenter, roofer, or electrician receives a new union contract for higher wages, the cost of new home construction goes up. When the cost of new houses goes up, so does the cost of existing houses. This is one reason why the value of residential real estate has more than doubled during the last 10 years.

Another reason is that as the land available for new construction becomes scarcer, the cost of that land goes up proportionately.

Other factors contributing to increased real estate prices are rising costs of borrowing money, governmental red tape, growth of control ordinances, and increased demand caused by the influx of new residents. This expanding population requires housing. Then, to serve this increasing population, retailers and service industries begin building new stores, an action that puts even more pressure on real estate prices.

You must face inflation as a fact of life. The house you find today, even at what seems to be an outlandish and historically high price, will cost much more in the future. Where investment in real estate is concerned, it's never too late.

Besides inflation, income taxes also take their toll on the wage earner. Yet real estate that earns income can shelter wage earnings for most people, up to a certain point. (For more information on income taxes, see Chapter 10.)

RICHES FROM BORROWED MONEY

The avenue to riches is paved with borrowed money. In real estate, you not only profit from your own savings but also from the borrowed money of others. Regardless of how wisely you invest, you can't go very far on your own money. Imagine how few people could afford to buy a home today without the assistance of borrowed money!

Leverage

A leveraged buyout is the use of a small amount of cash to acquire a much greater value in assets such as real estate. Leveraged buyouts are the secret to harnessing the forces of capitalism.

Your profits from leveraged investments are compounded by the use of borrowed money. Without leverage (using only your own money), it's too difficult to earn a reasonable return on your investment. Zero leverage would be a full cash purchase, using all your own money. In a leveraged buyout of a property, you would have a small down payment and finance the balance of the purchase price. The less you have invested, the more leverage you have. Maximum leverage would be a purchase that is 100 percent financed.

Due to the impact of inflation, which helps to enhance the appreciation of real estate, getting as much leverage as you can when purchasing real estate offers you a much greater yield on invested dollars.

For example, take a $50,000 property purchased with a 10 percent down payment using 90 percent leverage, as opposed to buying the same property for all cash (zero leverage). Ten percent down represents $5000. Now suppose that a year later the property increased in value by 10 percent to $55,000. Because it appreciated $5000 and the investment was only $5,000, the return on investment is 100 percent.

If the same property were purchased for $50,000 *cash* and, as in the previous example, it increased in value to $55,000, the return on investment would only be 10 percent ($5000 divided by $50,000 = 10 percent). Better yet, if you could purchase the same property with a 5 percent down payment, instead of 10 percent, you would actually double your return on investment from 100 to 200 percent!

As you can see, the more leverage you use, the greater your return on investment will be.

Keep in mind that all big business operates on borrowed money. Even giant corporations, such as General Motors, which has an abundance of surplus cash, always finance their realty acquisitions to improve their return on investment through leverage.

In the beginning you cannot expect to emulate the mighty tycoons of big business, but you can imitate them on a smaller scale. Later in the book you will discover how to buy a home with little or no money down. Furthermore, you will learn how to use your first property as a foundation on which to acquire other properties.

You Can Do It All in Your Spare Time

You don't have to quit your present job. In fact, steady employment greatly enhances your opportunities for borrowing. Once you have attained numerous income-producing properties, then you can think about quitting your job.

BENEFITS OF HOME OWNERSHIP

Special stock market events, such as "Black Monday" (October 19, 1987), when the market crashed 508 points in one frantic session, have served to emphasize the enduring value of owning a home.

Most Americans prefer safe investments with good performance records. Housing is one of those standards of enduring value, and as a result, American consumers have most of their wealth invested in the homes in which they live. Investment in a home gives families a hedge against inflation and an opportunity to accumulate wealth for the future.

Compare two similar families, each with two working adults and one child, a $40,000 combined gross income, and $10,000 to invest. One family buys a $95,000 home, investing $10,000 in the down payment and creating an $85,000 first mortgage at 10.5 percent fixed interest for 30 years. The other family continues to rent a home at $700 a month and invests $10,000 in a certificate of deposit (CD), which earns 6 percent interest compounded quarterly.

Under the assumption that family incomes, rent, and the value of the purchased home all increase by 5 percent a year and inflation rises 4.5 percent, at the end of the first year the homeowner pays $2723 less in federal income taxes and the value of the home will have increased by $4750, compared to a $612 gain in the value of the renter's CD.

At the end of five years, the homeowner has paid $10,761 less in federal income taxes and the home is now worth $121,248, a gain of $26,248. Were the homeowner to sell the home and buy another of greater value, the gain would be tax-deferred. By contrast, the renter's CD would be worth $13,457 after five years (a gain of $3457) and would be taxable.

Table 1.1 illustrates the tremendous gains attained through home ownership. Also note the column, Equity Build-up, which benefits the homeowner as payoff of the loan occurs.

From the examples given in Table 1.1, the net gain of the homeowner after five years, compared to that of the renter, is a difference of $36,998 in favor of home ownership.

ODYSSEY OF A VAGABOND INVESTOR: HOW I GOT STARTED

I do it not only for the money; I do it for the gratification. I enjoy the transformation of a dumpy old house into a beautiful home. And I enjoy the freedom that investing in real estate offers.

Because teaching has always been my forte, I discovered my ultimate satisfaction is in writing instructional guides about my favorite subject—real estate. To see my pupils and readers achieve expertise at realty investing pleases me even more than does a great book review!

Now that you know where I'm coming from, allow me to take you where I've been; to share with you a brief history of properties in which I've invested.

Table 1.1 Renting Versus Owning

After One Year				
	Tax Deduction	Gain in Value	Equity Build-up	Taxes on Gain
Homeowner	$2723	$4750	$402	deferred
Renter	0	612	0	$171
After Five Years				
	Tax Deduction	Gain in Value	Equity Build-up	Taxes on Gain
Homeowner	$10,761	$26,248	$2478	deferred
Renter	0	3457	0	$968

Michigan

My first realty investment was in 1968, when I purchased a small trailer-home and land overlooking the Muskegon River in Big Rapids. I was a freshman in college, and with the help of a friend, Tom Chapman, we each put $500 down and bought both trailer and land for $5000. This property is important not because of its profitability (there was none; I sold out to Tom at cost), but because it introduced me to investing in real estate.

Later on I transferred to Michigan State University and, with the help of a small inheritance, I purchased two properties in Lansing. Actually, the small inheritance was $11,000, of which I squandered half in the stock market before I got smart and invested the remaining half in real estate:

Logan house. I bought it for $13,400 in 1969 with $1500 down, and the balance financed at 7 percent. I then rented it for $240 a month, netting $112 profit monthly.

Okemos house. I bought it for $29,400 in 1970 with $1,500 down, and arranged three loans for the balance. I rented five bedrooms for a total of $480 per month and lived in the sixth. I cleared $112 monthly in profit, and lived rent-free.

California

Upon graduation from college, I saw no future for me in Michigan, and winters there are unbearable. So I decided to seek my fortune in California.

Lake Arrowhead house. (A large custom-built chalet overlooking the lake, the property included furniture and a boat). I purchased it in 1975 for $46,000 with no money down and 8.5 percent financing. Later I sold it for a $40,000 net profit.

Twenty-unit apartment building. In 1976 my partner and I bought this distressed property from a bank for $110,000 with $10,000 down, financing the balance at 8 percent. After extensive renovations and rent increases, we each earned $500 monthly after expenses. I considered this property the best money-maker I ever owned, as return on investment exceeded 100 percent.

Woodland Hills house. I bought this lovely home in 1980 for $95,000 with $5,000 down and assumed an 8.5 percent loan.

Nevada

In 1981, because of special business opportunities in Nevada, I sold off my remaining California property and moved to Las Vegas.

Meadowgrass condominium. In 1982 I purchased a cozy three-bedroom condo for $70,000 with $10,000 down and assumed the balance at 9 percent.

Biltmore house. In 1983 I bought a run-down two-bedroom house for $37,000 with $4000 down and assumed the existing 7 percent mortgage. Additionally, the seller accepted a note for the balance owing at 10 percent.

Arby house. In 1985 I purchased this beautiful custom ranch home sitting on a half acre overlooking the Las Vegas strip. The price was $96,000, $10,000 down and the balance financed at 8.5 percent.

Pleasant Road. In 1986 I bought another ranch-style home on a half acre for $88,000 with $15,000 down and assumed the existing first mortgage at 8 percent. In addition, the seller accepted a note for the balance owing at 10 percent. All four of these properties were successfully rented with the tenants having the option to buy, and I now net a total of about $1400 per month from them.

Florida

After eight years in Las Vegas and a serious case of casino burnout, I decided to move to Florida. I've always had a raging desire to own a home on the water with a boat parked out front. To me, Florida had the potential to realize that dream.

As of this writing, I have not yet purchased my dream home, only because the particular one I want is under construction. This special place is a condominium sitting on a bay overlooking the Gulf of Mexico. It has two bedrooms and two baths, a screened lanai, about 2000 square feet of living area, and as you have probably presumed, an incredible view.

Of course it has boat slips with access to the Gulf. It also has a restaurant and tennis courts, both essential because I enjoy eating out and I'm an avid tennis player.

My particular unit will be ready for occupancy in April, 1989. In case you're wondering how much it costs to live in paradise, the price is $110,000. Not too bad, but seven years ago the same thing would have cost $40,000. More importantly, seven years from now the same thing will cost $200,000 or more.

Finally, besides trying to write two books a year, I'm also involved in developing a magnificent parcel on the Gulf. My partners and I are trying to build 100 condos on a semi-developed waterfront site with 76 boat slips. Wish me luck.

But enough about me. My personal achievements are minuscule compared to the feats of certain other special people. Specifically I would like to share with you the story of my favorite person, who has been a great inspiration to me: Dr.

Jerry Buss, owner of the Great Western Forum and the renowned Los Angeles Lakers. Buss pyramided 700 small rental properties and parlayed them into a thriving entertainment showplace featuring the Lakers' magical showtime. He started with $1000 cash!

I hope that Jerry Buss will be as much of an inspiration for you as he has been for me.

IS REAL ESTATE RIGHT FOR YOU?

Although owning income property can be profitable and fun, it doesn't happen without a certain amount of work and effort on your part. I have prepared for you a complete guide to investing in real estate; however, it is you who must implement the ideas presented. You are required to do the following: locate the right property in which to invest, negotiate its purchase with the seller, locate tenants, collect rents, handle improvements and repairs, and prepare your income tax returns to maximize tax shelter benefits.

It is you who must determine whether you're capable of doing these things. They are the drawbacks of owning income property. Now consider the advantages.

On average, improved real estate will appreciate at one-and-a-half times the rate of inflation. That's right . . . 1.5 times the increase in the cost of living. Thus you have a super hedge against inflation.

Not only, then, is inflation on your side as a real estate investor, but time is also. As time passes, rents can be increased, which means that the property that had little or no cash flow when you bought it, can later develop positive cash flow from these rent increases.

Many property owners who have been fortunate enough to hold on to their properties *for a long time* are able to live off the net rental income. In other words, it is unlikely that income property purchased today with a small down payment will soon net a substantial positive cash flow. Yet as time passes, the property appreciates and rents are increased gradually, which over the long term will produce a substantial net income for the owner. Therefore, the longer you own the property, the greater will be your net income. And during the time of ownership, you enjoy the tax shelter benefits from the property. The point is: *Buy all the income property you can when you're young, then enjoy the income benefits when you're older.*

Besides the benefits of appreciation, growing income, and tax shelter, you also have a tremendous refinancing benefit. You can periodically refinance your holdings as the market value of your properties increases. Every few years you can refinance certain properties, pulling out cash to reinvest in more properties or do whatever else you want with the money.

Another method of income production occurs when the owner of real estate decides to sell. After owning property for an extended period, the owner will realize a sizable gain from the sale. He or she has the option of taking all cash from the gain or of accepting a note for equity in the property. This is ideal for retirees who quit their jobs and sell their properties, carrying the financing on a installment sale and enjoying the income from those monthly checks.

Variations on how real estate can provide income for its owner are almost boundless. It's the objective of this section to show you how to acquire at least $18,000 income annually from your realty investments. But this $18,000 is based on today's dollars. If inflation averages 6 percent a year for the next 20 years, you'll need three times as much—an unbelievable $54,000—to do what you can do this year for $18,000.

Based on the assumption that you can earn 12.5 percent in real estate on your cash investment, you'll need eight times (12.5 percent being one-eighth of 100 percent) $54,000, or $432,000 in equity by the twentieth year of your working life.

These projections contain a lot of assumptions and $432,000 in equities probably sounds like an unattainable goal, especially if you're just getting started. However, this is a step-by-step guide. First you start with one property; it will be the foundation for future realty investments. Later in the book you'll discover a wealth of profitable investment strategies that far exceed the 12.5 percent return on investment we've just discussed. Furthermore, you'll learn how to pyramid your investments in order to achieve your ultimate goal.

STEP-BY-STEP PLAN TO HALF A MILLION

"A journey of a thousand miles must begin with a single step." A famous Chinese proverb, certainly relevant to retiring on your acquired real estate. That's because a great achievement such as financial freedom doesn't just happen overnight. It's actually a carefully planned adventure.

You start with buying a home. It probably won't be your idea of a dream home, but for now you can call it home. More importantly, it will be the foundation of your inevitable financial freedom. As time passes, the undervalued home you purchased will be worth much more than you paid for it. And you've accumulated much equity build-up as the mortgage pays down. You've also been able to save on income taxes, because of interest and property tax deductions.

Now the home you bought a few years ago is completely renovated, and you're ready to do something with it. You could sell it, but real estate is better as a long-term investment. So you rent out the house, giving you supplemental income and tax relief. You buy another house, move in, and start remodeling it. After a few years, you rent it, and buy another.

Your long-term objective is about half a million dollars in equity, which is the amount you'll need for comfortable retirement. But to reach such a level of achievement, you must begin with the first step—purchasing your first home. Once your first home is acquired, it gets much easier to buy additional properties. That's because once you own the first home, it's easier to accumulate wealth. (The appreciating house, mortgage payoff, and income tax deductions all contribute to accumulating wealth.)

For a more detailed explanation of wealth accumulation, see Chapter 9, Pyramiding your Investments.

Finally, if you agree that investing in real estate is right for you, and that inflation is eroding your purchasing power and net worth, then I offer you a set of guidelines to make inflation work for you—instead of against you.

2 GETTING STARTED: A GUIDE TO RETIRING "ON THE HOUSE" DURING STAGES OF A LIFETIME

Are you aware that if you retired today at age 65, with maximum Social Security benefits, you'd receive only $899 monthly? To repeat, this figure represents *maximum* benefits. Most retirees could expect substantially less. That's hardly adequate for someone who envisions a laid-back retirement in paradise.

If you're assuming that your Social Security benefits and pension will be enough, or that you will win the state lottery, or that you will receive a large inheritance, you are probably not facing up to financial reality.

If you have the desire to retire comfortably "on the house," as most people do, you need a strategy with certain attainable long-term as well as short-term goals. That strategy changes according to age and family responsibilities. This chapter looks at five essential phases of your financial life, and at what steps you can take during each phase to eventually retire "on the house."

GETTING STARTED IN YOUR TWENTIES

Thinking about retirement is probably the last thing on a young person's mind. Perhaps you're just out of college or the

---

THE TWENTIES AT A GLANCE

- Begin with a budget
- Open a savings account
- Develop good bill-paying habits
- Avoid frivolous spending
- Set realistic goals, such as purchasing a home

---

military service. Your first real career job doesn't pay you much, but it's a good place to build experience. Now is the time in your life when it's easy to develop bad habits. You probably feel underpaid and are burdened with the usual after-college expenses: apartment deposit, student loan payments, and new clothes for your job.

Later on, after proving yourself on the job, you can expect your salary to increase. But for now, you really have no control over your salary. Until you're better compensated, it's very important to develop good financial habits and avoid certain common mistakes many young people make.

Avoid Common Mistakes

The biggest mistake you can make when you're young is to bury yourself in consumer debt. This includes credit card debt and new car financing.

Credit cards can be a useful asset, especially if they're used properly. In fact, building a solid credit history is essential to future utilization of sound real estate financing techniques. But credit cards can be a financial hazard if you misuse them.

Interest rates on credit cards average 18 percent. If you run up the balance to the maximum available credit limit, you're that much further behind in the quest for financial freedom. For now, it's wiser to decrease credit card debt at 18 percent rather than to put money in a savings account that pays 5 percent. Then, once a zero balance is attained, keep it that way by limiting your credit card purchases and paying off the entire balance when billed, thereby avoiding interest charges.

Everybody likes a new car, particularly young people. Yet payments on a new car are a drain on the family budget, as is the higher cost of insuring a new car. And don't forget that on average, a new car will lose 25 percent of its value once it's driven off the showroom floor. Not only that, but finance charges on a new car loan mean you end up paying about $20,000 for a $10,000 car.

It's wiser to keep the car you have, for as long as you can. After a few years, most depreciation has already occurred. By keeping it, and properly maintaining it, your car will be less of a drain on your budget, instead of an expensive toy that depreciates in value.

Another mistake some young people make is maintaining a leaky wallet. Sit down and make up a budget in order to plug the leak. Money seems to disappear into thin air unless you know where it's going. Get out a pencil and paper and detail how much money is coming in—items such as salary, tips, interest. Then, determine what it's spent on—such as rent, car payments, entertainment. You will be surprised at how much you are spending on items you can probably do without.

Consider packing a lunch to take to work. A savings of just $20 a week means an annual savings of over $1000. Also, think about car-pooling to work, or dining out less often.

Another big mistake young people make is getting involved with "get rich quick" schemes. In the hope of overnight riches, many young beginners opt for risky investments. Instead, you should set an initial goal of saving enough money to buy a home.

To complete your budget, list the value of your assets (savings, vehicles, furniture). Deduct your debts from your assets; the result is your net worth. Your goal is to gradually build your net worth through savings.

Set Realistic Goals

Financial freedom and a laid-back retirement do not happen overnight; they are created—by establishing realistic goals and attaining them through careful planning.

It is a step-by-step process. Start with a goal of saving enough money to purchase a home. Next, purchase the home. The long-term objective is half a million dollars in realty equities. But that's 15 years down the road, and you get there by careful planning and achieving one goal at a time.

Three to four years after buying your first home, you'll invest in an income property, which will be your third goal.

But for now, think about your second goal, which is the purchase of a home. To achieve this goal, you first have to accomplish goal number one.

Goal one is saving for a down payment to purchase a home. In addition to this amount, you also need at least three months' living expenses held in reserve for that unexpected rainy day. This will help to protect you should you find yourself unemployed.

When you're young, it's often difficult to save money, especially when you're barely meeting monthly expenses. This is the time when it's important to develop proper financial habits. Be disciplined. Start saving at least 10 percent of your gross income. If you can't save 10 percent, save 5 percent. If necessary, have the money automatically withdrawn from your paycheck. Saving $40 a week adds up to $2080 annually.

Once you buy the home, especially if you're single, consider renting out a room to help defray housing costs. You can earn $250 or more per month in additional income by renting out a portion of your home. In addition, because your home is now a rental, you can depreciate that portion which is rented, resulting in an added tax benefit.

Purchasing a home will be the wisest investment you could ever make. Eventually, not only will it be a source of pride and gratification, it will also be the foundation of your future financial success.

Finally, as part of developing good financial habits, be sure to maintain good bill-paying and banking habits. Good credit is necessary to purchasing a home (and keeping it) while maintaining the long-term mortgage, as well as to your quest to retire "on the house."

GETTING THERE IN YOUR THIRTIES

Now that you have grasped the essentials, you're probably discovering that life is becoming more complicated. You're still considered young in your thirties, but the clock is ticking and middle age is approaching. Life *is* becoming more complicated.

If you haven't already started your own family, you might be at least thinking about it. You also have to think about life insurance, a possible career change, or—if you have children—how to pay for their education.

The choices themselves have become more complicated. What types of insurance policies do you choose? What kinds of investments should you make? It is this time in your life when careful planning is absolutely essential.

The following is a guide on how to get serious with your financial future during your thirties:

THE THIRTIES AT A GLANCE

- Purchase a home
- If home is already owned, invest in additional rentals
- Read up on real estate, business, and finance
- Save for children's education
- Eliminate non-mortgage debt

Own a Home

If you don't already own a home, it's time to buy one. If you do own a home, then it's time to begin looking for income property in which to invest. (Chapters 3 and 5 in this book will show ways to purchase a home, some with no money down.)

Control Living Expenses

People in their thirties, especially those experiencing greater incomes than they had in their twenties, tend to want bigger and more expensive things. They feel that they've outgrown the existing home, and that it is time to live it up with a new, big, expensive home. This could be a big mistake, because this age is the time in your life when control of living expenses is imperative.

Instead of thinking about an expensive new car parked in front of your country estate, you should be thinking about protecting your loved ones and planning for your children's education. Later on, after you have accumulated more wealth, will be an appropriate time to enjoy the more expensive fruits of life.

Insurance

To protect your family, the less-expensive term insurance is preferred. Other forms of investment insurance, such as whole life and variable life, offer cash build-up, yet they have high premiums and low death benefit coverage. Under term insurance, premiums pay only for death benefits.

How much term insurance should you get? A good rule of thumb is: enough that the death benefit, if invested conservatively at a reasonable yield, would generate sufficient income to replace your paycheck.

Prepare a Will

Protection for your family also means being prepared. This means having a will that stipulates the disposition of your assets after your death. If you have children, be sure to spell out in the will who you want to be responsible for them should you and your spouse die. Otherwise, the courts will decide who inherits your assets and raises your children.

Save Money by Cutting Living Expenses

You need investment money to make intelligent real estate purchases. But how can this extra money be obtained? If you're buried in consumer debt, even though your spending habits are already spartan, look at ways to cut fixed costs. Credit-card debt, on average, costs about 18 percent. But a home equity loan might cost 11 percent. Therefore, consider replacing more expensive credit-card debt (which is only partially tax deductible until 1991) with an equity loan (which is tax-deductible, not to mention 7 percent less in interest charges). If you have any loan proceeds left over after paying off the credit card debt, consider investing it in income property.

You can also save money by owning just one car. Don't be afraid of downward mobility if it means gaining control of your finances.

ALTERNATIVE METHODS TO SAVING MONEY

If the company you work for has an employee pension plan, consider investing surplus cash in it. The most common retirement plan, the 401(k), allows you to contribute up to 25 percent of your gross wages, up to $7313. If you're in the 28 percent tax bracket and contribute the maximum, you save $2048 in income taxes. And in some cases, your employer adds 50 cents for every dollar you contribute, up to 6 percent of your pay.

If the 401(k) or other type of retirement plan is not available, consider an Individual Retirement Account (IRA). You can contribute up to $2000 annually and in the 28 percent tax bracket, that's a savings of $560 in income taxes. Contributions to an IRA are fully deductible if neither you nor your spouse is eligible for a pension plan, or if your adjusted gross income is less than $25,000 for singles, $40,000 for couples. In addition, even nondeductible contributions enjoy tax-deferred compounding until withdrawn beginning when you are at least age 59.5. However, IRAs do have certain drawbacks. They have limited liquidity and you have to pay penalties for premature withdrawal.

If you're self-employed or the owner of a small business, look into a Keogh plan. It's designed for small businesses with 25 or fewer employees. As the owner/employer, you're entitled to tax-free contributions of up to $30,000 annually.

Prepare for Child-Raising and College Costs

If you don't have children already but would like to have them, you'd better start financial planning now. Having a child not only means loss of spousal income during maternity leave, but also medical and nursery-furnishing costs. If you decide to have a child, try living on one spouse's paycheck before the birth of your child, and put the other paycheck into savings.

Before you know it, your toddlers will be starting college. The sooner you set up a college savings plan, the easier it will be when the costs of tuition, books, and rent begin. Whatever they cost today, in twenty years they will probably cost three times as much.

You have to decide whether to save money in your own name or in your child's name. Under the child's name, the earnings benefit from a tax break; however, you lose control of the money when the child is no longer a minor. Most financial planners recommend keeping the account in your name.

Recent changes in the tax law offer help for college savers. Interest from U.S. Savings Bonds purchased after 1990 is tax-free if the bonds are used to pay for college. Here's how it works: You have a child who will be starting college in 12 years. After January 1, 1990, you invest $500 in a savings bond. The bond will be worth $1000 when it matures in 12 years. Of the $500 in accumulated interest, normally you'd owe federal (but not state or local) tax on it. But if the bond is used for a child's college education, you'll pay no tax.

To qualify, the bond investor must have the bond in his or her name and be older than age 24. In addition, the tax exclusion applies only to couples who have joint taxable incomes of under $60,000. After 1990, this income limit will increase based on the rate of inflation.

You should start reading about such subjects as real estate, business, and finance. In this way, you keep abreast of interest rates and the latest methods of earning money on tax-free investments. This information is valuable to an up-and-coming homeowner and investor. Recommended reading is the money section of the newspaper USA Today, especially the Monday edition.

GETTING THERE IN THE FORTIES AND FIFTIES

THE FORTIES AT A GLANCE

- Buy income property from an equity loan
- Maintain emergency reserve and adequate insurance
- Control spending
- Work at eliminating non-mortgage debt

THE FIFTIES AT A GLANCE

- Continue buying income property
- Target retirement date
- Check on expectations from pension and Social Security
- Check out potential retirement sites
- Work at eliminating mortgage debt

During your forties, try and think of yourself as halfway around the rack track, with the home stretch in sight. Your home or other investment property, its value fattened by inflation and years of mortgage payments, is likely your prime source of investment capital. As mentioned earlier, a home equity loan is ideal for paying off costly credit card debt. In addition, the proceeds from an equity loan can be used very profitably as investment capital.

Borrow the Maximum Against Your Home

Borrowing against the equity in your home is especially beneficial during inflationary times. When you obtain a long-term, fixed-rate loan during periods of inflation, you're able to pay back the long-term obligation with dollars worth less than those you borrowed. In other words, as inflation continues to erode the purchasing power of the dollar, over time the debt is paid back with dollars that are worth much less.

To illustrate this, if you had taken out a loan against your home in 1967 over a 30-year term, you'd still be making payments on it today. However, today's loan payments are made with dollars worth only 34 cents compared to the dollars you borrowed 21 years ago. (Based on the Consumer Price Index, one dollar in 1967 is worth 34 cents in 1988.)

Granted that you would have paid interest on the borrowed money ever since 1967, yet the rate of interest would have been at a fixed rate of 6 percent, which is much less than what you would pay to borrow money today. And this interest cost is further reduced by its tax-deduction benefit.

How much economic benefit you receive from borrowing against the equity in your home depends primarily on what you do with the loan proceeds. You get maximum benefit by paying off costly credit card debt with a less expensive equity loan that's tax deductible. Then, with the balance of the loan proceeds, invest in additional income property on which you can obtain appreciation and tax shelter benefits—gains that exceed the value of leaving the cash as equity in your home.

Avoid Keeping Excess Cash in Savings

As an active real estate investor you should look at a savings account as a temporary depository for emergency cash, not as a permanent haven for large amounts of capital.

Yes, you can earn 5 percent or so in a savings account, but if inflation is averaging 6 percent you're actually losing one percent annually, and that's before you pay income taxes. The interest earned is taxed at either 15 or 28 percent, depending on your tax bracket. If you're taxed at the higher bracket, the net yield on a 5 percent account (after taking inflation and taxes into consideration) is a negative return of 2.4 percent.

Control Spending

During your forties (and thirties), especially if your careers have progressed gradually, there's a tendency to try and keep up with the Joneses. Some might feel they've earned the right to own a big, expensive home and car. Yet this is the time when you could be blowing one of life's great opportunities to build net worth.

By now, your monthly housing costs begin taking a smaller and smaller share of monthly income. It happens very slowly—as you get pay raises and earn more income from rental properties, while your housing expenses remain relatively fixed.

Instead of an unwise move into a more expensive home, consider adding to the existing one, especially if your family has outgrown it. You'll benefit later in higher resale value.

Besides housing expenses, you can control other spending by trimming the fat from your budget. Avoid buying luxury cars, unless you've already got college costs and retirement under control.

Once you're retired and the kids are no longer a financial burden, there will be plenty of time to spend money on the more material fruits of life—if you have the money to spend.

THE FIFTIES: APPROACHING THE HOME STRETCH

These are your peak earning years. If the house isn't paid for yet, soon it will be. The kids are out on their own, which means they're no longer a financial burden. Retiring "on the house" is just a short time off—even sooner if you can swing it.

This is the time in your life when expert financial planners recommend saving at least 20 percent of your gross income. If you're not saving at least this much, you need to take certain steps to increase your savings rate.

One step is to charge room and board to any live-in boarders, such as adult children living at home who are capable of caring for themselves. Otherwise, they'll drain your finances.

Another step is to avoid interest costs. Pay cash for a used car, instead of financing a new one. Also, limit your vacation and leisure time budgets. In other words, be thrifty now so you can retire more comfortably later.

Pay Down Mortgages

You can save thousands of dollars over the life of a mortgage by prepaying it. The savings might surprise you, and you'll especially benefit on income property after the loans are paid off (by earning more cash flow).

For example, consider a $75,000, 30-year fixed-rate mortgage at 10 percent. Add $100 per month to the $658 payment, and you'll pay it off in 17.5 years and save $78,000 in interest charges.

The sooner you start prepaying a mortgage, the more you'll save. That's because of the structure of a typical amortized mortgage. During the mortgage's early years, most of your payment is applied to interest, while a small portion is applied to principal. To illustrate this: Of the first $658 payment, $625 is applied to interest and $33 to principal. Even after you pay on the mortgage for 12 years, the payment is split $549 for interest and only $109 for principal.

Prepaying the mortgage can be as simple as writing a note to the lender, saying that the extra amount is applied "to principal." If you think about it, you're trading 17.5 years of prepaying the mortgage at $100 monthly, in order to save $78,000 in interest charges. In other words, you prepay $21,000 over 17.5 years to earn $78,000 in savings.

Secondary financing on income property can also be prepaid. For example, consider a property purchased with a second mortgage on it: When you bought the property, you arranged a second mortgage with the seller for $30,000 at 10 percent interest, amortized over 10 years at $397 per month.

Currently the property is rented, and because of paying on the second mortgage, you receive no positive cash flow. (The income from the rented property equals the expense.) You could prepay the second mortgage by $100 per month, which results in paying off the second mortgage in about half the time. Thus you could time the early payoff of the second loan to coincide with your retirement date. This would not only save you thousands of dollars in interest, you also earn $397 more in monthly income at a time when you could really use it.

During your fifties you need to change your strategy for certain types of investments. This means switching from aggressive growth to preserving assets and generating cashflow or income. To this end, dump volatile or speculative stocks. Also, sell off unproductive real estate, such as undeveloped vacation land.

Although later in this chapter I recommend renting a home when it comes time to retire, there is an exception. Buying a vacation home years before retirement can offer you a number of benefits. By investing in a vacation home you'll save money on vacations. Bear in mind that you'll be retiring in a few years. After retirement, you'll have plenty of time to travel. For now, enjoy your vacations in your second home, and save vacation dollars doing it. It's a place to relax, to enjoy fixing up, and to dream about living there full-time someday.

By having a vacation home you'll also benefit psychologically by knowing you'll have a home when you retire. You ease the transition to retired life. That's because by arranging the retirement home now, you avoid the stress related to the move later on.

Furthermore, although investing in vacation property and renting it when you're not there usually doesn't produce positive cash flow, in most cases it does offer appreciation and tax-deduction benefits.

Rev Up Realty Investments

If your realty holdings are already sufficient for a comfortable retirement, then you only have to switch to a preserving-assets mode. But if your current real estate holdings are inadequate, then you need to be a more aggressive investor. To this end, you have to learn to make use of accumulated equity.

Over time, unless you properly utilize accumulated equity in income property, you'll be faced with a *diminishing return on equity dollars*. It's important to understand the principles involved. As you'll see, there's a point at which equity build-up causes the rate of return on equity to fall substantially below the rate you earned during your early years of ownership.

Take, for example, an apartment building I bought several years ago for $110,000, with a $9000 down payment and $3000 invested in renovating it. My first year's equity position, before appreciation, was $12,000. After one year, when all improvements were completed and rents increased, the fair market value of the property was $135,000. So in the second year of ownership, my new equity position equaled the initial investment of $12,000, plus the increase in property value of $25,000, or a total of $37,000.

Return on equity is determined by dividing annual net income by equity in the property. Since first-year net income was $5400 and equity was $12,000, return on equity during the first year was 45 percent.

During the second year, net income remained constant at $5400. But since the property appreciated $25,000, my equity position increased by that much to a total of $37,000. If $5400 is divided by the higher equity position of $37,000, the result is a return on equity during the second year of 14.6 percent.

As long as the property continues to appreciate, the return on equity dollars diminishes year after year. This diminishing return occurs because the equity build-up is stagnant. It's just sitting there without being reinvested, until I convert this equity to another investment (which I can do by trading or selling it, or taking out an equity loan).

It's often wise, especially if you're an aggressive investor and have obtained a substantial equity position in the property, to make use of that equity. In doing so, you'll avoid a diminishing return on accumulated equity.

Project Retirement Income

The first place to check is your place of employment. Find out how much you can expect from your pension plan.

On Social Security, you can check the status of your account by calling the Social Security Administration (SSA). Call the U.S. Department of Health and Human Services and ask for card number SSA-7004, a request for statement of earnings. You can also obtain the card directly by writing to SSA, P.O. Box 57, Baltimore, MD 21203.

Check Out Possible Retirement Sites

Consider using your vacations to investigate potential places where you might want to live. But before you make a hasty decision, collect your thoughts and consider what kind of climate you like, how far you want to move from family and friends, how important shopping and restaurants are, what you need for health care, and what cultural or sporting activities suit you.

While vacationing, talk with the people who live and work there. Also, find out what rents and real estate prices are, as well as state and local income taxes, property taxes, and sales tax. All these levies vary substantially from state to state, and they can take a big chunk out of a fixed income.

Finally, get your estate in order. Be sure your will is up-to-date. Failure to draft a will leaves your estate open to administration. If your wishes are not made explicit, litigation is more likely; the family has to endure delays of up to one year and thousands of dollars in unnecessary court costs. Furthermore, if your inheritable assets exceed the $600,000 exempt from estate taxes, hire a capable lawyer to set up a trust agreement. In fact, your attorney might find it advisable to recommend a trust even if your estate does not exceed this amount.

THE SIXTIES: A GOLDEN TIME TO ENJOY

THE SIXTIES AT A GLANCE

- Update health and life insurance
- Reduce financial risk
- Eliminate debt
- Sell or convert realty holdings to property management company
- Kick back and enjoy the fruits of your labor

Probably the greatest fear of a future retiree is the thought of losing everything you worked for—to the health-care costs of a prolonged illness. If you're close to retirement, check with your employer to find out if you can extend health insurance coverage when you stop working.

Another alternative is Medicare supplemental health insurance. For more information on this coverage or other sources, check with the American Association of Retired Persons (AARP).

Regarding life insurance, the older you get, the more expensive it is. The less-expensive term insurance is better at this stage of your life. Get enough coverage so that the death benefit, invested at a conservative rate of return, would generate sufficient income to replace current earnings.

Reduce Risk

The sixties are a good time to switch your investment strategy from *aggressive* to *safe*. Think diversification and income. Certificates of deposit are ideal for retirees. They're secure and liquid and help replace your salary. Senior adults shouldn't concern themselves with long-term gains in the value of assets. Also, if your portfolio is big enough, consider high-quality tax-free municipal bonds.

Eliminate Debt

Too much debt can psychologically wear you down. A laid-back retirement means enjoying the fruits of your years of labor, and not being hassled by debt collectors. If possible, pay off the principal residence mortgage, credit cards, and other loans.

IRAs

The earliest you can begin withdrawing (without penalty) from an IRA is at age 59.5. The latest is April 1 of the year following the year in which you turn 70.5. The minimum distribution depends on your life expectancy, or the joint life expectancy of you and your beneficiary.

Sell or Convert Realty Holdings to Property Manager

If you plan to relocate after retirement, more than 300 miles away, you'll either have to sell all your realty holdings, or turn the responsibility of managing them over to a competent property management company. Don't even think about trying to manage them yourself while living such a distance from your assets. It's just not practical. You need someone to handle repairs, collect rent, and show vacancies. These tasks are better handled by a competent person living in the geographical area of your holdings.

Invest in CDs

If you decide to sell your realty holdings, the best thing to do with the proceeds is to buy one-year CDs. Purchase them in chunks of $50,000 or more. Most financial institutions offer their best rate on $50,000 and above. Invest your CDs in different institutions, so as not to exceed the $100,000 FDIC insurance limit.

To find the best CD rates, check the ads in the business section of local newspapers and the *Wall Street Journal*. Be sure your CDs are insured by the FDIC or FSLIC. Both are U.S. government agencies that insure deposits up to $100,000.

Time the purchase of your CDs so that they mature every month or two throughout the year. Then you can simply roll over (reinvest) each CD when it matures, or spend the money however else you like.

Kick Back and Enjoy the Fruits of Your Labor

Retirement can be the best time of your life. Think of it as a new and exciting phase in your life, with time to do the things you want to do. Happy and contented retirees enjoy themselves. They do it by contributing and learning, rather than just killing time; actively golfing, fishing, and playing tennis, rather than just moping around; by writing a book or making a speech, rather than sitting in front of a TV; by cherishing friends and loved ones, rather than being ornery and bitter; by realizing that retirement is the beginning of a new and exciting stage of life—rather than the end of an old one.

Now that you have a grasp of getting it together during stages of a lifetime, let's look at ways of getting the most for your money through financing real estate.

PART TWO
Buying Your First Property

3 FINANCING REAL ESTATE

It's critical for you to understand the principles of financing real estate—even before you get into other key areas such as property evaluation, profitable strategies, and negotiating. Financing real estate is a subject of paramount importance.

If you're confused about the maze of financial terminology and the variety of loans used in today's sophisticated real estate market, don't be discouraged. You don't need to be an expert. You only need to be informed of the various alternatives; then you can select the best type of financing for your particular needs.

This chapter takes you on a step-by-step journey through this maze of financing, offering you a clear and concise description of the current loan types being issued throughout the United States. I use many examples to illustrate the effect of selecting one type of mortgage over another, graphically showing you both positive and negative aspects of each loan type.

The greatest mistake a real estate investor can make, other than overpaying for a property, is paying too much for the wrong financing. Since the most important segment of investing in real estate is predicated on the financing itself, I've allotted considerable space to this crucial subject.

Important Note

Before we discuss financial terminology and all the various loan alternatives, the best advice I can offer comes in a double dose: 1) Always assume low interest rate loans (instead of originating new financing) whenever you can; and 2) if you do have to originate new financing, always arrange fixed-rate financing (as opposed to adjustable-rate). There are two exceptions to this second dose. They are: 1) Adjustable-rate financing is only advantageous to the borrower if the loan is held four years or less; and 2) if the adjustable-rate loan is convertible to a fixed rate during the first four years. (More details on this subject are discussed later in this chapter.)

The following material will cover, in detail, the various financing alternatives, including financial terminology.

FINANCIAL TERMINOLOGY

Before going any further into the realm of finance, you should become familiar with some of the more common financial instruments and terms.

Mortgages and Deeds of Trust

Mortgages and **deeds of trust** are financial instruments that create liens against real property. These instruments state that, should the borrower default on the loan (fail to make payments when due), the lender has the legal right to sell the property in order to satisfy the loan obligation in a foreclosure sale.

There are two parties involved in a mortgage: the **mortgagor,** also called the borrower and property owner, and the **mortgagee,** also called the lender. There are two parts to a mortgage: the **mortgage note,** which is evidence of the debt, and the **mortgage contract,** which is security for the debt. The note promises to repay the loan, while the contract promises to convey the property's title to the mortgagee in case of default.

Trust deeds are similar to mortgages except that a third party is involved and the foreclosure procedures are simplified. Under a trust deed, the borrower/owner is called the **trustor.**

The lender is referred to as the **beneficiary.** The third party, whose responsibility is to hold title to the property for the security of the lender, is called the **trustee.**

Under a trust deed, if the trustor defaults on the loan obligation, the subject property may be sold at public auction by the trustee through the "power of sale" clause contained in the trust deed. This public auction may take place *without court procedure.*

(Please note that although these foreclosure proceedings are most common throughout the country, some variations in procedure may occur state to state.)

Foreclosure is initiated by a notice of default, which is recorded by the trustee with a copy sent to the trustor. If after three months the trustor does nothing to remedy the situation, a **notice of sale** is posted on the property, and advertisements of the sale are carried in local newspapers once a week for three weeks. If during this period the trustor fails to pay the beneficiary sufficient funds to halt the foreclosure, the sale will be conducted by the trustee. Proceeds from the foreclosure sale are first disbursed to the beneficiary, then to any other lien holders according to their priority.

Foreclosure under a mortgage instrument, as opposed to a trust deed, takes substantially longer (periods in excess of a year are common).

Second trust deeds and mortgages (or thirds, fourths, etc.) are similar to firsts, except that they are second in priority to a first loan with respect to security and their ability to claim any proceeds from foreclosure sales.

Differences Among Assumed, Subject-To, and Transferred Mortgages

There are important differences in the meaning of these terms. An *assumed mortgage* occurs when the borrower assumes the legal obligation to make the loan payments, while the lender releases the previous borrower from this liability. Assumption, then can only legally take place *in the absence of a due-on-sale clause* (defined below).

Buying the property **subject to** the existing mortgage occurs when the buyer takes over the loan obligation without the existing borrower being released from the liability, and without formal arrangement with the lender. Caution should be taken when buying property subject to an existing mortgage—especially when a due-on-sale clause is involved—because the legality of enforcement of the due-on-sale clause differs from state to state.

An **assigned (transferred) mortgage** is one that you already own. It is an asset or a negotiable instrument that has value. It is also a note on which someone is paying you principal and interest, and your security is the mortgage against certain real property. As your down payment, you could assign (transfer) this mortgage to the seller of the property that you wish to acquire.

Also, be aware of **due-on-sale** and **alienation** clauses written into loan documents. Without going into great detail, they both mean essentially the same thing; that is, if the title transfers to another party, the lender can either call the total amount owed due and payable within 30 days, or he/she can ask for assumption fees and an increased rate of interest. FHA and VA loans do not have these clauses, which makes these loans very attractive, especially if the interest rate is below the market interest rate. They are also attractive because they are fully assumable in most cases, without any credit qualification whatsoever.

Points

A **service point** represents 1 percent of the loan amount. These service points, often called loan origination fees, are incorporated into the loan with the purpose of increasing the lender's yield without raising the interest rate. As an example, a lender might quote a 30-year fixed-rate loan at 10.5 percent, plus 2 points. This means that in order for the lender to originate such a loan, the borrower must pay 2 percent of the loan amount (2 points). What lenders charge in service points tends to fluctuate as do interest rates, according to the supply and demand of money available to lend.

MORTGAGE ALTERNATIVES

In today's sophisticated mortgage market, the key to profitable real estate investing is selection of the right loan. More than $30,000 can be saved over the loan's term, on the average purchase, when the borrower is informed of all the types of loans available, and then is careful to utilize the best loan attainable.

All the mortgage alternatives will be listed in order of preference to the borrower. Thus, mortgage assumption is first; VA loans are second; FHA loans are third; and conventional financing is last.

Originating any type of new loan is both costly and time-consuming. Typically, originating a new loan entails loan origination fees of about 4 percent of the proceeds, and often requires more than two months to complete the transaction. Furthermore, the borrower is faced with paying the going market rate of interest for the loan.

So, what are the alternatives for the prospective realty purchaser, and how can he/she efficiently borrow money to make profitable realty investments?

Loan Assumption: The Best Alternative

Loan assumption is, by far, the best method of financing real property for a number of reasons. But before we consider these reasons, there are two exceptions to loan assumption's preferred status. Loan assumption is not economically feasible when the existing interest rate (which will be assumed) is higher than the prevailing market interest rate for mortgage loans. The second exception is when you're considering the purchase of newly constructed property; if that is the case, only the creation of new financing is available to the buyer, because the builder usually has to be cashed-out from an unassumable loan position.

Therefore, if your potential real estate purchase is not a new home, consider assuming existing low-interest-rate loans. They have the following advantages:

1. You can save up to 4 percent of the loan amount in origination fees by assuming an existing loan, as opposed to originating a new loan. (On a $100,000 loan, that amounts to $4000 in savings, not to mention the additional savings earned by the assumptor in lower interest charges over the term of the loan.)
2. If you assume existing VA, FHA, or certain adjustable-rate loans (and in some rare cases, conventional loans), you will not have to qualify. This means there will be no

credit report or questions asked. In other words, you don't need good credit.

3. Not only are assumable loans attractive from a buyer's point of view, but when you sell, your buyer can assume the same loan—which makes your property much more saleable because of the built-in financing.

4. Instead of allowing the buyer to assume your valuable low-interest-rate loan, you could also create a new wrap-around loan—and make a profit from the spread in interest rates between it and the underlying loan. (More details on wrap-around loans are available later in this chapter.)

VA Loans

Another alternative, second in preference to loan assumption, is the creation of new financing backed by the Veteran's Administration (VA). Qualified veterans can borrow up to $144,000, with no money down, at an interest rate usually one point below that of conventional financing.

To apply, the qualified veteran is required to submit a copy of his or her form DD-214 to the VA. If approved, the VA will submit a certificate of eligibility to the veteran; the certificate is then issued to the loan underwriter. The VA guarantees the loan, up to a specified amount, against default by the veteran.

VA loans that originated prior to March 1, 1988 are fully assumable without buyer qualification.

FHA Loans

Third in preference, behind loan assumption and VA loans are loans insured by the FHA. The FHA insures lenders against loss, and offers home buyers loans up to $110,000 with about 5 percent down. The typical FHA loan is usually one point below the cost of conventional loans. Existing FHA loans are fully assumable, with one exception: FHA loans that originated after January 1, 1987 require that the assumptor's credit be reviewed if the loan being assumed is less than two years old (one year if the property is owner-occupied) and if it originated after January 1, 1987.

Conventional Financing

Real estate loans are divided into two categories: loans insured or guaranteed by federal government agencies, such as the VA and FHA and occasionally, state government and loans that are not. Loans without government support are termed *conventional* loans.

Conventional financing is the least-preferred way to finance real property. This is primarily due to the cost of such loans. Typically, the borrower must make a 20 percent down payment. A smaller down payment is possible, but the additional cost of private mortgage insurance (PMI) at about 0.5 percent is then applicable.

Besides the higher down payment requirement, conventional terms require the borrower to pay the prevailing market rate of interest (usually 1 point higher than that of similar VA and FHA loans). In addition, the conventional lender charges up to 4 points in fees, which include the cost of loan origination, appraisal, and credit report.

As you can see, you can realize tremendous savings by acquiring the proper financing. Just the reduction of one point in interest rate can save you thousands of dollars over the life of a typical home loan, plus additional savings when you avoid costly loan origination fees. Finally, most conventional loans are unassumable; this means that the sale of your property is inhibited, because a new loan will be needed in order to acquire the property from you.

TYPES OF REPAYMENT PLANS

Real estate loans can be classified in several different ways. One means of classification is according to the plan of repayment of the loan (the borrower and lender must agree on this). The basic repayment plans available are:

- Interest-only (straight-term) loans
- Fixed-rate amortized loans
- Adjustable-rate mortgages (loans)
- Graduated loans

Interest-Only Loans

Also known as the straight-term loan, it requires the payment of interest only during the term of the loan. At the end of the term, the entire sum of principal is due and payable in one final "balloon" payment. For example, the annual payment schedule for an interest-only loan for $12,000 at 10 percent interest for a term of five years is $100 per month ($12,000 × .10 divided by 12 = $100). At the end of five years, a "balloon" payment of $12,000 will be due and payable.

Prior to the Great Depression of 1929–1939, the interest-only loan was the most common payment method for real estate financing. Many borrowers took out these loans for short terms expecting to renew them term after term, thus deferring almost indefinitely their repayment of the principal.

But the entire world economy failed during the Depression, and most lenders were unable to "roll over" (perpetuate) these interest-only loans. The results were devastating. Lenders began calling in loans, requiring borrowers to pay the entire principal amount owing, a sum which most borrowers didn't have. Then, as a consequence, lenders throughout the country began foreclosing on these loans.

Although Risky, Interest-only Loans Can Be Profitable. Interest-only loans can be risky. But if used properly, they do have certain advantages. Take, for example, an interest-only loan of $20,000 at 10 percent payable in 10 years at $167 monthly. The risk involved with this type of loan, unlike the fully amortized loan, is the balloon of $20,000 owing after 10 years.

By committing yourself to a $20,000 balloon, you're assuming that you'll be able to pay it off when it's due. In 10 years, it would seem likely that the equity to which the loan is tied—the house—will have appreciated. At that point, you could refinance the existing loans and pay off the $20,000 balloon.

But what if interest rates are high when it's time to refinance? Or what if the house hasn't appreciated much in 10 years? These are the risks of obligating yourself to a balloon payment.

An interest-only loan on $20,000 at 10 percent for 10 years is $167 monthly, which equals the monthly cost of interest. The same loan amortized over 10 years is $264 monthly, with a zero balance owing at term's end. Thus you could earn $97 monthly ($264 − $167) on income property by paying less in loan payments, but you'd have a glaring obligation of $20,000 staring you in the face in 10 years.

The Depression made almost everyone, especially in the financial industry, aware of the dangers inherent in interest-only loans. A more practical form of loan soon materialized: the amortized loan.

Fixed-Rate Amortized Loans

The fully amortized loan features a fixed rate of interest with equal payments, consisting of both principal and interest, over its term. In contrast to the interest-only loan, the fully amortized loan commonly has a longer term (20 or 30 years) and is completely paid off at the end of its term.

Initial payments on the amortized loan consist mostly of interest; but as the loan matures, more of each payment is applied toward principal, since interest on an amortized loan is calculated on the loan's outstanding principal balance. Therefore, after each payment is made, the principal balance owing is reduced, resulting in a smaller interest portion and a larger principal portion of the overall payment.

Table 3.1 illustrates how a fully amortized loan at a fixed rate of interest is paid off over its term.

Fixed-rate amortized mortgages commonly have 30-year and 15-year repayment terms. As with all fully amortized loans, the initial mortgage payments are mostly for interest; this portion gradually becomes less as the loan pays down. But with a shorter-term loan such as the 15-year, a larger amount of principal is paid (especially in the beginning). Table 3.2 shows accumulated equity after 5-, 15- and 30-year periods.

You also save on the cost of interest. Most of the savings

**Table 3.1 Example of How a $5,000 Loan Is Amortized at
10 Percent for 5 Years**

Loan Balance	Interest (Monthly)	Loan Balance & Interest	Payment	Principal (Monthly)	Payment No.
5000.00	41.67	5041.67	106.24	64.57	1
4935.03	41.13	4976.56	106.24	65.11	2
4870.32	40.59	4910.91	106.24	65.65	3
4804.67	40.04	4844.71	106.24	66.20	4
4738.47	39.49	4777.96	106.24	66.75	5
4671.72	38.93	4710.65	106.24	67.31	6
4604.41	(loan balance after 6 payments)			395.59*	

Note how monthly interest is added to the loan balance, then the regular monthly payment is deducted, resulting in a new loan balance.
*Accumulated equity (principal) build-up after six payments.

occur due to the shorter term of the 15-year mortgage, although the lower rate of interest is also helpful.

Table 3.3 shows required monthly principal and interest payments for a $70,000 loan at various selected rates of interest at both 15 and 30 years. Don't forget that 15-year loans have a slightly lower rate of interest, usually 0.5 percent lower, than do 30-year loans.

Adjustable-rate Mortgages (ARMs)

Adjustable-rate mortgages (ARMs) originated around 1980, in order to protect long-term lenders from radical changes in market interest rates. Traditionally, conventional lenders loaned their funds at reasonable fixed rates, and rightly so, as their cost of acquiring that money seldom fluctuated. But along came the hyper-inflationary times of the mid-1970s and 1980s, and the cost of money to lend increased dramatically. At the same time, lenders had billions of dollars loaned out at interest rates substantially below what it cost them to acquire these funds. Hence the arrival of the adjustable-rate mortgage.

ARMs vary somewhat, but basically they work in similar ways. The interest rate of the loan is allowed to fluctuate over

**Table 3.2 Comparing Accumulated Equity and Interest Paid on
15- and 30-Year Loans**
(Contract interest rate of 10 percent; loan amount $70,000)

Time	15-Year Accumulated		30-Year Accumulated	
	Interest Paid	Equity Earned	Interest Paid	Equity Earned
After 5 yrs	$32,044	$13,090	$34,479	$2380
After 15 yrs	65,401	70,000	97,766	12,810
After 30 yrs	—	—	151,152	70,000

the entire term of the loan. Usually, if the interest rate origi-
nates at 9 percent, it is allowed to increase up to 6 percentage
points to a maximum limit of 15 percent, with a maximum
increase of 2 percent during any 12-month period.

Typically, the amount of interest charged the borrower is
tied to some index rate such as the prime rate. In other words,

**Table 3.3 Comparison of 15- and 30-Year Loans at
Selected Rates of Interest (Loan Amount $70,000)**

Interest Rate (%)	Payment Required 15-Year Loan	Payment Required 30-Year Loan
8.0	669	514
8.5	689	538
9.0	710	563
9.5	731	589
10.0	752	614
10.5	774	640
11.0	796	667
12.0	840	720
13.0	886	774
14.0	932	829
15.0	980	885

if the prime rate goes up, your ARM interest rate goes up (but not to exceed 2 points in one year, and not to exceed 6 points over the term of the loan).

Usually a borrower can originate an ARM at a lower interest rate than that of a conventional fixed-rate loan, mainly due to less risk incurred by the lender. However, the borrower must realize that the interest rate of the ARM may increase 6 points over its term. For instance, on a loan of $80,000 at 8 percent for 30 years, the principal and interest payment would be $587.02. For the same loan and term at 14 percent (the 6 percent maximum increase allowed), the principal and interest payment would be $947.90, a monthly difference of $360.88. Over the entire term of 30 years, that's a difference of over $129,000. As you can see, ARMs represent a substantial and significant risk to the borrower, and with the sole exception of a very short-term loan, it would be wise to avoid them.

I mention the one exception of a short-term loan. Studies have shown that ARMs are more cost-effective if only used during the short term. In fact, 4 years is the break-even point in comparing the ARM to a fixed-rate mortgage. In other words, if you plan on maintaining the loan 4 years or less, the ARM is less expensive than the fixed-rate; if you plan to maintain the loan more than 4 years, then the fixed-rate mortgage is more economical.

Convertible ARMs

A convertible ARM is the latest innovation in real estate financing. This is an ARM that can be converted into a fixed-rate loan, with the lender setting certain limits relating to the conversion. At the time of this writing, initial offerings of the convertible ARM consisted of convertibility at a cost of $250 to $750 to a fixed-rate during the first five years of the loan's term. The initial rate of interest is 8.75 percent plus 2 points, compared to 10.5 percent plus 2 points on a 30-year fixed-rate loan.

How ARMs Work

The adjustable-rate mortgage's interest rate is allowed to change (along with your monthly payment) every one, three, or five years. The period from one rate change to the next is called the adjustment period. Thus, a mortgage with an adjustment period of one year is called a one-year ARM.

Rate Change Limits. The interest rate on an ARM is tied to an index. When the index rate moves up or down, so do your payments at the time of adjustment. There are limits, however, on how much your interest rate can change at any one time and over the life of the mortgage. The interest rate change is usually limited to a maximum of 2 percent during each adjustment period, and an overall cap is placed on the interest increase.

Most lenders use indexes tied to some easily monitored rate, such as the U.S. Treasury securities rate. The lender applies a margin to the index used.

Margins. The margin is an amount added to the index rate to produce the interest rate to be charged the borrower. A margin is applied to all ARMs and usually varies among lenders.

One lender may charge the Treasury index plus a margin of 2 percent; another lender may use the same index plus a margin of 3 percent. Thus, after your first period of adjustment, one lender's offering would be 1 percent cheaper, based on the amount of margin applied. For example, the difference between 11 percent and 12 percent on a $70,000 loan is $53 per month. Over a 30-year term, that amounts to $19,080, which is a substantial saving to the borrower who can acquire the lower rate of interest.

Margins are an integral part of competitive pricing of mortgages. They reflect the lender's cost of doing business and their resulting profit.

The margin, the index, and the adjustment period are the essential subjects to discuss when you shop for a mortgage. Besides comparing margins among lenders, you also have some choices about the frequency of your rate adjustments. Keep in mind, however, that lenders will charge a higher rate for longer adjustment periods.

Safeguard Features. Many lenders offer certain caps, or specified limits, on rate increases (or monthly payments) in any adjustment period or over the term of the loan. Most ARMs have both payment caps and interest-rate caps.

Payment Caps. A payment cap sets a ceiling on how much your monthly payment can increase in any one year. This provision protects you from excessive increases when market interest rates go up.

Interest Rate Caps. Interest rate caps limit the increases in the interest rate itself. These caps come in two varieties:

1). Caps that limit the amount of increase in interest rate from one adjustment period to the next, and

2). Caps that limit the amount of increase in interest rate over the life of the loan.

These caps act to insure the borrower. Like other forms of insurance, you have to pay to get them; how much you pay depends on each particular situation.

You are now aware that the payments on ARMs can move up or down depending on interest rates within the economy. Specifically, what happens if interest rates stay the same or decline? If interest rates stay the same, then—as a rule—your payments will stay the same. If interest rates decline, your payments will likewise decline, as they have in the recent past. In June, 1982, the interest rate on a one-year ARM was 16 percent; in June, 1983, the rate declined to 12 percent. This means that the monthly payment on a $70,000 loan would have been reduced from $942 to $720.

There is much to consider when choosing an ARM. Remember that lending money is a highly competitive business; lenders in your area may offer different features on ARMs as they compete for your business.

Important Note About ARMs

Generally speaking, the long-term trend of interest rates is up. However, interest rates occasionally experience short-term declining trends. Borrowers who chose ARMs in 1982 have paid substantially less in interest than those who got fixed-rate loans; yet this period of declining interest rates is insignificant in comparison to the overall rising trend.

Interest rates follow a directional trend over an extended period, then usually change direction and begin a new trend. Seldom are they stable. The best way to determine the direction of future rates is to make an educated guess and go with the trend.

Fixed-rate loans are better for the long term, and for periods when interest rates are rising. The reason: You lock in your rate and don't have to worry about increases, as you would when the ARM comes up for adjustment.

Graduated Loans

Also known as the graduated payment mortgage (GPM), this plan offers smaller initial loan payments which become larger as the term of the loan goes on. The graduated loan anticipates the borrower's future ability to repay the loan; specifically, the plan assumes that the borrower's income will grow to meet the GPM's schedule of increasing payments.

This type of loan has two inherent drawbacks. The first is the increasing payments over the term of the loan. This could be disastrous to the borrower if he or she is unable to increase his or her income to meet the higher demands of increasing loan payments. The second drawback is negative amortization. Negative amortization is the opposite of amortization (paying off the loan). In other words, instead of the principal balance being reduced after each payment, it actually increases. Thus, the borrower can actually owe more than he or she actually borrowed after making several loan payments.

Due to these drawbacks inherent in this type of financing, both the VA and FHA have eliminated the GPM under their current loan programs. The reader should likewise avoid these types of loans.

SPECIAL TYPES OF FINANCING

Besides the VA, FHA, and conventional financing, the potential investor has several other methods available with which to finance real estate. Under certain circumstances, the seller of the property can also be the lender, as when the property is sold under a wrap-around mortgage or land contract. The following material covers these unique and innovative methods of financing, as well as some others.

Wrap-Around Mortgage

The "wrap," also called an all-inclusive trust deed (AITD), is a unique and innovative method of financing real property. But note that only assumable loans (those without due-on-sale clauses) can legally be wrapped with a new all-inclusive mortgage. And bear in mind that in order for a wrap to be profitable, the underlying loan(s) must be at a low fixed rate of interest. This is because you will want to wrap the existing low-interest-rate loan(s) with a new higher-rate loan, and earn the profit in the interest rate spread.

This lucrative method is also ideal when you have a large amount of equity in the property. Here's how it works:

In Figure 3.1, the seller creates and carries a new loan of $110,000 at 11.5 percent. Payments on the existing first and second loans are a total of $850 per month. Payments on the new wrap are $1050 per month; therefore, the seller earns a $200 per month profit.

As you can readily see, there are tremendous advantages to

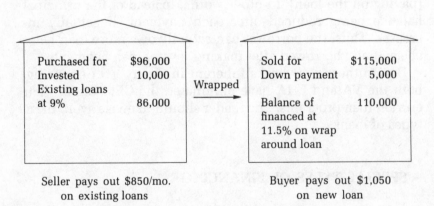

Purchased for	$96,000		Sold for	$115,000
Invested	10,000	Wrapped	Down payment	5,000
Existing loans at 9%	86,000	→	Balance of financed at 11.5% on wrap around loan	110,000

Seller pays out $850/mo.
on existing loans

Buyer pays out $1,050
on new loan

Figure 3.1 Wrap-Around Loan Example

assuming existing low-interest-rate loans. Besides the cash savings in acquiring these loans, their flexibility allows you to wrap them and earn a handsome profit. Just the fact that you have all this built-in financing on the property is reason enough to avoid creating the other, more cumbersome forms of new financing.

Advantages to the Seller of the Wrap. Under the wraparound loan the seller receives a higher return, as opposed to allowing the buyer to assume the existing low-interest-rate loans and to carry back a loan for the seller's equity. Also, the seller is likely to receive a higher price for the property under a wrap, through favorable terms (buyer is not required to pay loan origination fees, or pay for appraisal and credit report costs).

Advantages to the Buyer of the Wrap. Under the wrap, the buyer can acquire property with a small down payment without paying for loan origination fees, appraisal, and credit report. Furthermore, the wrap saves time that would otherwise be required to shop and apply for a new loan, and the buyer is only responsible for one loan payment.

Precautionary Measures for Protection of Buyer and Seller. There are two such measures:

1. Seller should retain the right to approve the credit of all subsequent buyers in the event that the property is resold.
2. To avoid the possibility of the property being lost in foreclosure due to failure of the seller to make payments on the existing underlying loans, a neutral trust (such as a title company) should be made responsible for receiving payments from the buyer, and then for making underlying loan payments for the seller. Costs of such an arrangement, as well as who pays those costs have to be considered.

Purchase-Money Second Mortgage

This is a method of financing in which the seller of the property takes back a loan for the equity in the property, instead of taking cash. The key is for the seller to have a large equity position. In this way the seller is lending you his equity, which you pay off over time at below-market interest rates.

Suppose, for example, you buy a house for $80,000 with a $5000 down payment, and you assume an existing $50,000 loan. The $25,000 balance remaining is carried back by the seller in the form of a purchase-money second mortgage payable under terms you negotiate with the seller. In this example, $30,000 represents the seller's equity in the property. You pay $5000 down, and instead of $25,000 cash, the seller takes back a purchase-money second mortgage of $25,000 (see Figure 3.2.).

Terms on the $25,000 purchase-money second mortgage are very negotiable and can take shape according to the needs of both buyer and seller. Typically, purchase-money seconds have an interest rate of 10 percent; however, this rate is negotiable. Of course, the lower the rate of interest you can negotiate for yourself, the better off you'll be. I've seen sellers retain second mortgages as low as 8 percent, and as high as 12 percent. (Some states have usury laws which prevent excessive rates from being charged. You should find out if your state has these laws.)

Purchase-money seconds are an integral part of profitable real estate investing. This is because you can create inexpensive seller financing which, in most cases, can be assumed by the next buyer. You can actually earn more money by keeping your interest rates low, and then reselling your properties at higher rates.

Price		$80,000
Assume existing first mortgage	$50,000	
Down payment	5,000	
New purchase-money second mortgage	25,000	
Total	$80,000	

Figure 3.2 Example of Purchase-Money Second Mortgage

As an example, a few years ago I found a great property that, at first glance, seemed impossible to buy with a small down payment, nor was it likely that the seller would carry back any financing. This gorgeous property had an existing 8 percent first loan of $40,000, and the seller wanted $25,000 down. The asking price was $119,000, and the seller's agent doubted that the seller would be willing to carry back a second loan.

Not to be denied, I made an offer of $92,000; I would pay $10,000 down and assume the existing first loan of $40,000, and the seller was to carry back a second loan at 9 percent for the balance owing of $42,000. Neither my agent nor the seller's agent believed this offer had a one-in-a-hundred chance of being accepted. But to everyone's surprise the seller made a counteroffer of $96,000 while accepting all the financing terms of my offer. Thus the only change from my offer was the increased price, from $92,000 to $96,000, which also increased the amount of the second loan carried back—from $42,000 to $46,000. I gladly accepted the counteroffer.

Here's an illustration of that transaction:

Purchase price		$96,000
Assumed first loan	$40,000	
Down payment	10,000	
New purchase-money second	46,000	
Total	96,000	

In this example, I created $46,000 in new low-interest financing on a property that, at first glance, you'd have thought would never sell under such advantageous terms. Six months after I purchased this lovely money-maker, I sold it for $115,000 on a wrap-around mortgage, and I was to net $350 or more per month on it for the next 20 years. The reason I say "or more" is because once the underlying second loan is paid off, which will be in about 9.5 years, I can continue to collect on the wrap without having to pay on the second loan.

There are two primary reasons for this property's profitability: 1). I sold the property for $19,000 more than I paid for it; 2). Due to the low-interest-rate loans that were maintained after the sale (8 percent on the first and 9 percent on the second), I collected 11.5 percent on the total balance owing for the next 20 years.

Based on this experience, you never really know whether a seller will carry back a note unless you at least attempt to create low-interest secondary financing by making a legitimate offer.

Take-Out Seconds

A take-out second loan, also called an equity loan, is different than a purchase-money second loan in that it's created from equity in property already owned. For example: You own a property with $50,000 equity in it. You could take out a second mortgage against that equity to make home improvements, pay for a college education, or buy additional income property. Usually, institutional lenders fund this type of loan in amounts up to 80 percent of your equity in the property.

Take-out seconds are probably the most expensive method of financing real estate and substantially reduce your equity in the encumbered property, although they can be favorable under certain conditions. Here are two situations when a take-out second can be advantageous to the borrower:

- A take-out second could be better than refinancing if the existing first mortgage has a below-market rate of interest. (See Chapter 13 for a more detailed look at refinancing versus taking out a second loan.)
- There is a tax loophole for equity loans; the Tax Reform Act of 1986 created it. According to this law, the consumer-interest deduction is being phased out, yet certain equity loans are tax deductible. In other words, because of changes in the tax law, it would be reason enough to take out an equity loan just to pay off all existing consumer debt (which is not tax deductible) with new equity debt (which is tax deductible).

Land Contracts

A land contract, sometimes called an installment contract, contract of sale, or contract of deed, is strictly a contract between buyer and seller without the involvement of a financial intermediary. Under a land contract a buyer agrees to purchase a property and pay principal and interest to the seller, along with an optional down payment. Title to the property remains with the seller until conditions of the contract are fulfilled. The buyer retains possession of the property; however, if the buyer should default on the agreement (not pay as agreed), the property would revert to the seller.

Similar to a wrap-around mortgage, land contracts are useful in "wrapping" existing low-interest-rate financing. The agreement should stipulate that the buyer pays a certain fixed rate of interest, which to be profitable must be higher than the combined rate on the underlying loans. Furthermore, it's advisable that a neutral trust be arranged, for protection of both buyer and seller. In this way the buyer makes payment to the trust, which in turn makes payments on the underlying loans, taxes, and insurance. The remaining part of the buyer's payment is then remitted to the seller.

Caution must be taken when structuring buyer and seller conditions in a land contract; the law covering this subject is vague, and the status of land contract sales varies from state to state. Therefore, before involving yourself with this form of financing, consult a trusted attorney.

Equity Sharing

Another method available to finance your purchase is equity sharing (also known as shared equity, equity participation, equity partnership, and shared appreciation). This concept originated out of the need to pair cash-short buyers with cash-rich investors. The buyers and investors share ownership of the property, and both gain later when the property is sold, if it is sold for a profit.

Here's how it works. Let's say you're short of cash to make a down payment on a home, and your parents want to help. Your parents would agree to make the down payment in exchange for one-half interest in the house. You agree to occupy the house, maintain it, and pay fair market rent to your parents for their interest in the property. You and your parents split the costs of principal and interest, property taxes, and insurance. Because they are rental property owners, your half-owner parents can claim income tax deductions of mortgage interest, property taxes, and depreciation. (If your parents had simply made the down payment in the form of a gift, they would receive no tax or appreciation benefits.) Your tax deductions will be the same as for all homeowners, that is, deductions for mortgage interest and property taxes.

Taking title to a property under equity sharing is usually the same as purchasing a home on your own. Both parties go on the title (consult local statutes) and both parties sign the mortgage note and take responsibility for its payment.

Equity-sharing transactions require one additional step. A written agreement between co-owners is necessary to precisely spell out important points such as ownership percentages, rent to be charged, buy-out options, resale specifics, and responsibility for repairs and maintenance. The agreement should also specify procedures in the event of death, default, disability, bankruptcy of a co-owner, or "acts of God" (such as floods, earthquakes, and tornadoes).

Equity sharing, then, can be beneficial to both the investor and the owner/occupant. The owner/occupant can eventually buy out the investor, sell the house, and use the proceeds for a down payment on another house. The investor gets a tax advantage from the ownership interest of a rental property, and can share in its appreciation.

No-Money-Down Strategies

There are a number of methods that can be used to finance a property with nothing down. Each particular situation will require a different approach, usually depending on the seller's cash requirements, and the assumability of the existing loan(s). Please note that closing costs are ignored in the following no-money-down strategies.

Seller Requires No Cash. If the seller requires no cash and there is an existing assumable loan, then the buyer can simply assume the existing loan and have the seller carry back a second loan for the remaining balance of the purchase price. Obviously, this is the least complicated method of acquiring real property with no money down. But now let's look at another situation, the only difference being that the seller will not carry a note and wants to be entirely cashed out.

Seller Needs to Be Cashed Out. For the purpose of example, you locate a house that can be bought for $60,000, and there exists an underlying $50,000 VA loan (which the seller will allow to be assumed). If the seller needs to be cashed out, there are two alternatives: 1). You could borrow the down payment of $10,000 and assume the balance owing, or 2). You could avail yourself of a somewhat more complicated alternative, which involves discounting a note. Here's how it works:

The problem to resolve is how the seller can obtain cash for the $10,000 equity interest in the house. One method would be to convert the $10,000 note to cash. But to convert a note to cash usually requires that the note be discounted. This is because the typical investor requires more of a yield than a common purchase-money second normally yields (about 10 percent).

Let's say an investor will buy the note at a 25 percent discount. If this is so, the holder of the note would only receive $7500 in cash for the $10,000 note.

But what if the seller requires the full $10,000 for his equity interest, and won't accept the reduced amount of $7500? The solution is to increase the note's value to $13,333 and discount it 25 percent, which would yield the required $10,000.

Therefore, in order for the seller to receive cash for the $10,000 equity in the property, the seller would have to carry back a $13,333 note. The note could then be sold to an investor at a 25 percent discount, and the seller would receive the required $10,000. (We arrive at these figures by a simple algebraic calculation: We divide the reciprocal of the 25 percent discount, which is 75 percent, into $10,000; the result is the amount of the note required which, when discounted, yields $10,000.)

Obviously, this solution requires the buyer to pay a premium for the property, in this case an additional $3333. However, paying a premium isn't all that bad, as long as one is not overpaying for the property; and, because the property is purchased with no money down, the investor obtains maximum leverage.

Six-Month Rollover 100% Financed. This strategy is based on the theory that an all-cash purchase commands a bargain price and that the seller is highly motivated to sell. It involves paying all cash for property, all of which is borrowed, then quickly renovating the property and reselling it at a profit. When the property is sold, the borrowed money is immediately paid back, and the seller earns a profit.

For example, let's say you've located a property which, if purchased for $67,000 cash and renovated, could be sold within six months for $100,000. For the purpose of this example we will presume that you have a lender that will lend you $72,000 for six months. Figure 3.3 will illustrate how the numbers work.

From the example given in Figure 3.3, the finance cost is calculated as follows: In today's market a financial institution would usually fund such a loan, including renovation costs, at 14 percent plus 4 points. Loan proceeds consist of $72,000, of which $67,000 represents the purchase price while $5000 is the cost of renovation. Therefore, interest on $72,000 for 6 months is $5040, plus 4 points at a cost of $2880, for a total of $7920. Although this financing cost may look excessive, this investment strategy supports the cost because of the great profit potential, especially considering that this technique does not require any of your own funds.

If you have enough ready cash to use the six-month rollover strategy, without borrowing the required working capital, then you'd be even further ahead—because you'd save $7920 in finance charges.

The sales commission is another optional cost which was included in this analysis. Due to the short time period involved in this method, I usually find it necessary to pay a commission to procure a quick sale. However, if you can make a sale without the services of an agent, you would save an additional $6000.

Purchase price		$67,000
Less the following expenses to acquire and renovate		
Closing costs	$ 500	
Cash to renovate	5,000	
Cost to finance	7,920	
Tax and insurance (6 months)	300	
Utilities (6 months)	200	
Total expenses	$13,920	
Total expenses and purchase price		$80,920
Property is sold for		$100,000
Less the following selling expenses		
Sales commission (6%)	$ 6,000	
Closing costs	500	
Total expenses and purchase price	$80,920	
Total overall expense		$87,400
Net profit before taxes		$ 12,580

Figure 3.3 Six-Month Rollover 100% Financed

Ingredients of the Six-Month Rollover. The key to this investment strategy, assuming the working capital is to be borrowed, is to have a lender tentatively in place for such a transaction. Then, once you locate a property in which you wish to invest, you would make an offer contingent upon acquiring sufficient financing. If your offer is accepted, it would then be analyzed by your lender. Should the lender agree, you're in business. If not, the offer would be nullified because of the financing contingency inserted into the offer to purchase.

To profit from this innovative method, certain rules must be applied, and only certain properties qualify. You can use this rule of thumb when planning to use the six-month rollover strategy: If you buy it at no more than two-thirds of its selling price after it's renovated, you make a good deal. For instance, in the example in Figure 3.3, the purchase price was $67,000, which is two-thirds of the selling price of $100,000. If you purchased a home for $80,000, the selling price would have to be $120,000 to incorporate the two-thirds ratio.

Properties that best qualify are those that have a substantial amount of equity, and on which the seller is unwilling to carry back a note; they require much renovation, yet are sound in structure and overall construction. A large amount of equity usually means that the seller has owned the property for an extended period. Since he or she bought the property years ago for substantially less than what it's worth now, and is unwilling to carry a note or renovate the property, he or she would be inclined to sell at a bargain price in order to be totally cashed out.

A final word: When you buy a property and intend to sell it within one year or less, you can earn substantial savings on the cost of title insurance. Most title companies will allow you to pay a retainer, usually $50, which will be the total cost of title insurance when you sell. The cost of such a policy without the retainer is about $500. Thus you can save $450 by paying the retainer in advance, when you purchase the property.

QUALIFYING FOR A NEW LOAN

When you finally think you're ready to ask for a loan, stop—take a deep breath—and prepare yourself for quite an ordeal, especially if the loan you want is government-backed. Conventional loans usually can be processed in 30 days; VA and FHA loans can take from 60 to 120 days. (Bureaucratic red tape and additional inspections usually add to the time required on government-backed loans.) However, you can help speed up the approval process by carefully obtaining and submitting information required by the lender.

When you initiate the loan request, the lender will first have you fill out the loan application. If you have all the pertinent information required on the loan application, go ahead and fill it out completely. If not, take the application home, fill it out, and either mail it or return it personally to the lender.

In addition to the loan application, you must sign an employment verification form; the lender will then submit it to your employer. You should alert your employer to the coming inquiry.

If you are self-employed, you must supply the lender with federal income tax returns for the past two years, and a profit-and-loss statement since your last tax filing.

From the information on the loan application, the lender will order a credit report. Once the credit report is made available to the lender, he or she will scrutinize it carefully. If your credit is not approved, you will be informed of the bad news.

When the lender receives the appraisal and title report, he or she will analyze both, then determine the maximum amount he/she will lend on the property. Next the lender takes into account your income, to see if the monthly payment falls within stipulated guidelines. (Remember, a maximum of 28 percent of your gross monthly income is allowed for principal and interest, taxes, and insurance.) If it does, you will then be informed of this amount, as well as the number of points and the interest rate the lender will charge.

In certain cases, there are additional steps in the loan process. Under VA and FHA rules, a property inspection is required in order to determine whether the property meets certain minimum standards. Also, certain states require a termite inspection of the property.

How Much House Can You Afford?

The following material pertains to originating a new loan, as opposed to loan assumption. Note that although loan assumption does not require qualification (no questions asked), the borrower should still keep the loan payment within the guidelines suggested for originating a new loan, in order to avoid potential financial difficulties.

How much house you can afford depends on many things. Married couples with children can afford a certain amount; single people usually can afford to pay proportionately more of their income toward the purchase of a home.

As a rule, couples with children should not exceed 28 percent of their gross monthly income for the house payment, including the cost of principal and interest, property taxes, and hazard insurance. Single people and married couples with no children usually can afford up to 33 percent of gross income for a house payment.

Institutional lenders require a range of 25 to 28 percent of the borrower's gross monthly income as the limit for the house payment. This percentage, of course, can reflect a second income from spousal earnings. Professional lenders know from experience what it takes to avoid financial difficulties. Therefore, it is wise to maintain your payments within these limits, no matter how you acquire the loan.

Originating a new loan requires a down payment of from 5 to 20 percent of the purchase price, depending on where you get the loan (except for a no-money-down VA loan).

Conventional loans require a 20 percent down payment, 5 percent when private mortgage insurance (which costs about an extra 0.5 percent) is used. FHA loans require about 5 percent down.

Closing Costs. In addition to your down payment, you will have to pay certain costs at closing. As a rule, total closing costs average about 4 percent of the purchase price when you originate a new loan. The following are cost items that can show up on a closing statement (some of these charges may not apply to your transaction):

- *Loan origination fee.* Expect to pay at least 2 points of the loan amount to originate a new loan.
- *Loan commitment fee.* Expect to pay 1 point if you want to lock in a guaranteed rate at closing. If you accept the market rate at closing, you won't have to pay this fee.
- *Escrow fee.* This includes document preparation and notary services necessary to complete the transaction.
- *Appraisal.* This is a cost that the buyer customarily pays when originating a new loan.
- *Credit report.* This is a cost that every borrower pays in order to initiate a new loan.
- *Title insurance.* A title policy, usually issued by a title insurance company, assures payment to successful claimants in disputes about title to the property. The cost of this insurance is usually paid by the seller; occasionally it is split between buyer and seller.
- *Recording fee.*
- *Termite report.*
- *Prorated taxes.*

In addition to the above closing costs to the buyer, the seller is obliged to pay certain closing costs. They are:

- *Sales commission.*
- *Fees such as escrow, recording, reconveyance, and trust fund.*
- *Title insurance* (see also buyer's list above).
- *Points on government-backed loans.*
- *Prepayment penalty.*
- *Revenue stamps, either state or local.*
- *Transfer taxes.*
- *Prorated rents, taxes, and interest.*
- *Impound account.*
- *Documentary stamps.*

Closing Costs Summary. Generally speaking, creating a new loan will cost about 4 percent of the loan amount. This cost will include the incidental closing costs that pertain to your particular transaction. Bear in mind that a loan assumption can save you plenty of money. The assumption fee, by itself, is only about $50, and because you're not originating a new loan, you save the cost of 2 percent of the loan amount just in origination fees. You also save the cost of a credit report and appraisal, because these items are not required under a loan assumption.

Now that you have a conception of closing costs, see Tables 3.4 and 3.5 (which illustrate monthly payments at selected in-

Table 3.4 30-Year Fixed Monthly Payment (P&I) at Selected Interest Rates

Amount ($)	Interest Rate (%)								
	8.0	8.5	9.0	9.5	10.0	11.0	12.0	13.0	14.0
60,000	440	461	483	505	527	571	617	664	711
70,000	514	538	563	589	614	667	720	774	829
80,000	587	615	644	673	702	762	823	885	948
90,000	660	693	724	757	790	857	926	996	1086
100,000	734	771	805	841	878	952	1029	1106	1189

Table 3.5 15-Year Fixed Monthly Payment (P&I) at Selected Interest Rates

Amount ($)	Interest Rate (%)								
	8.0	8.5	9.0	9.5	10.0	11.0	12.0	13.0	14.0
60,000	573	591	609	627	645	682	720	759	799
70,000	669	689	710	731	752	796	840	886	932
80,000	765	788	811	835	860	909	960	1012	1065
90,000	860	886	913	940	967	1023	1080	1139	1199
100,000	956	985	1014	1044	1075	1137	1200	1265	1332

terest rates for both 30- and 15-year fixed-rate loans). Select the loan amount in the left column, then go across the top and select the appropriate interest rate. Where the loan amount and interest rate intersect is the computed monthly payment for principal and interest (P & I) which you will pay to amortize the loan.

Table 3.6 shows the monthly mortgage cost of borrowing per $1000 for both 15-year and 30-year fully amortized loans at different interest rates. As an example, if you wanted to know the monthly mortgage cost of a $12,000 loan at 11 percent for 30 years, you would first look at the 11 percent column. Then select the 30-year row; the factor is 9.53. To find your monthly payment on $12,000, multiply the 9.53 factor by 12, which results in a monthly payment of $114.36.

Loan Payments and Income Needed to Buy a $90,000 Home

Since the average home in the United States sells for about $90,000, here is a table that features the payment and income

Table 3.6. Monthly Fixed Payment (P&I) Cost Per $1000 at Selected Interest Rates

Term	Interest Rate (%)								
	8.0	8.5	9.0	9.5	10.0	11.0	12.0	13.0	14.0
15-Year	9.56	9.85	10.15	10.45	10.75	11.37	12.01	12.66	13.32
30-Year	7.34	7.69	8.05	8.41	8.78	9.53	10.29	11.07	11.85

required for a house costing that amount at selected rates of interest. Table 3.7 illustrates how much income you need to qualify to purchase a $90,000 house. The numbers are based on a $10,000 down payment and a financing of the remaining $80,000 at various fixed rates for 30 years. Annual property taxes and hazard insurance (T&I) are estimated at $120 monthly. Private mortgage insurance is not included, for simplicity. The total monthly payment, which includes principal, interest, taxes, and insurance (PITI), is based on 28 percent of the minimum qualifying monthly income.

Table 3.7 Loan Payments and Income Needed to Buy a $90,000 Home

Rate (%)	Monthly P&I	Monthly T&I	Total PITI	Annual Income to Qualify
8	$587	$120	$707	$30,000
9	644	120	764	32,743
10	702	120	822	35,229
11	762	120	882	37,800
12	823	120	943	40,414
13	885	120	1005	43,071
14	948	120	1068	45,771

SUMMARY

The adjustable-rate mortgage is a relatively new method by which lenders may overcome long-term unpredictability in the economic climate. Thus, all the risk of the unpredictable future is with the borrower (and no longer with the lender) under adjustable-rate conditions. Under fixed-rate conditions it is the lender who is at risk. Therefore, if you have to originate new financing, always try for a fixed rate; if you have to obligate yourself to an adjustable-rate loan, make it a convertible loan (one that can be converted to a fixed rate over five years). Also remember that ARMs can only benefit the borrower when the loan is maintained four years or less. Four years is the break-even point. If you maintain a new loan for more than four years, the fixed-rate loan is cheaper.

Don't forget the many advantages of loan assumption. Whenever you can, especially if you're just getting started in real estate investment, try to assume existing low-interest-rate loans. Not only are they hassle-free, but they're much cheaper; and you can even make a profit with them under a wrap-around loan situation.

Finally, you might be wondering exactly what is a reasonable amount of interest to pay. As a general rule of thumb, long-term mortgage interest rates become expensive or unfavorable at 10 percent or more. Anything under 10 percent is considered a favorable rate.

For now, this gauge of value works. What the future will hold depends on the volatility of interest rate movement. Those loans below 10 percent are valuable; they are cheap money. Keep this cheap money. Should hyper-inflationary times return, future mortgage payments will be made with cheaper dollars, benefiting the borrower. If interest rates rise, the homeowner can hang on to the below-market-rate loan; if interest rates plunge, the homeowner has the option to refinance.

4 KEY INGREDIENTS TO PROFITABLE OPPORTUNITIES

Profitable opportunities in real estate investment can be found in any city or town throughout the United States; you only need to develop an eye to spot these opportunities. Certain key ingredients usually have to be present in a potential realty investment in order to make it a superior buy. They are:

- An undervalued fixer-upper
- Acquisition of the proper financing
- A large equity position
- A motivated seller
- The more land, the better
- A good location in a thriving market

These are the six key ingredients for the greatest profit opportunities in residential real estate investment. If the property you purchase has all these qualities, you can be assured that you've made a sound investment. Now let's look at each ingredient in detail.

AN UNDERVALUED FIXER-UPPER

Fixer-uppers come in all shapes and sizes and degrees of work required to renovate them. The ideal candidate, especially for the beginner or the small-scale investor, would be a single-family residence (SFR) that simply needs cleaning up and some painting inside and out. Less ideal would be a similar house needing substantially more capital and work, such as new carpeting, roof repair, new kitchen, and bathroom tile.

But the amount of work required to renovate doesn't matter (as long as the building is structurally sound) if you're not on a limited budget. You can always profit on a fixer-upper as long as the value of the improvement equals twice the cost of such improvement and as long as you bought the property at a bargain price. If you have a limited budget, stick to investing in properties that require minimal amounts to renovate.

Two-for-One Rule

The rule of thumb for evaluating whether a property is worth fixing up is that every dollar invested in renovation should yield at least two dollars in increased property value. For example, you buy a house and spend a total of $4000 renovating it; you should be able to realize at least $8000 in gain after sale.

Properties become run-down primarily due to lack of adequate maintenance. Often the landscaping is overgrown; trash is strewn about, inside and out. The place probably stinks to high heaven, and there are a few broken windows. This shabby and unhealthy condition presents a great opportunity for the opportunistic investor. All the filth and destruction substantially reduces the value of this house. All you have to do is determine what it will cost to clean and renovate this property, and the price at which you can reasonably sell it and earn a profit.

SFRs: The Wisest Choice

There are two types of real estate investors: big and small. Big investors have become big by making small investments, accumulating wealth, and turning to bigger and better things—such as huge apartment buildings and shopping centers. Small investors are the rest of us—the ones who need more income, more tax shelter, more accumulated wealth, and the eventual achievement of becoming big investors.

For the small investor, specializing in SFRs is the wisest choice. There is a plentiful supply of SFRs with much demand. There are many small investors and first-time home buyers who create this demand. For a typical middle-income family, home ownership is definitely the number one priority.

The category of SFR does not include condominiums. Condos only represent 10 percent of the overall residential market, and thus lack the adequate demand of the public at large.

But why specialize at all? A medical doctor specializes in one particular field of medicine and an attorney specializes in one particular field of law because he or she is an expert in that particular field. It's much more practical, and probably easier, to be an expert in one field than to become a jack of all trades, master of none.

If you stick to learning about SFRs, values in the surrounding neighborhood, typical selling prices, and costs per square foot of homes throughout your city, you can succeed as a real estate investor. That is because all you really need to know is how to recognize a good buy, how to fix it up, and what it will sell for.

How Do You Know If a Property Is Undervalued?

To be a successful real estate investor, it is essential that you evaluate potential investments accurately. You have to know how to recognize a bargain when you see it, determine how much it will cost to renovate, and then determine at what price you can honestly sell it. Determining value, then, is the "nuts and bolts" of investing in real estate. Without proper appraisal techniques you could be faced with the primary pitfall of real estate investment: paying too much for your property.

But you can easily overcome this pitfall by learning the local market. Once you know market values in your geographical area and know the selling prices of properties, you can more efficiently locate and purchase a sound investment.

The first priority in making an accurate appraisal is to know the market where you plan to invest. It is not only important to know the prices at which properties have sold, but also to be informed of *asking* prices. Without adequately knowing the market, it will be impossible for you to accurately determine value. Therefore, to become knowledgeable about local real estate values, start by doing your homework. Obtain a Multiple Listing Service (MLS) book from your friendly realty agent to get a feel of what's available, and at what price, in your area. Look up recent sales in the MLS book, and especially take note of the price-per-square-foot and raw land values.

Price per square foot is the most important factor in quickly determining the value of improved property. From your research in the MLS book, determine the price range at which property in your area sells (at price per square foot). From this information alone, you can usually determine whether a property deserves further attention. For example, if you already know that you can sell a particular home at $50 per square foot of living space, you can be assured that if you buy it at $40 per square foot or less, you will have made a good buy.

You should also become familiar with unimproved land values. What is the value of a vacant standard-sized residential lot or a half-acre lot in your area? This information will become very important later on in your investment career. Remember, you're better off with more land. If you don't have enough land, you won't be able to add on to the house or build a guest home on the property—additions which would substantially add to the value of the property.

Besides using the MLS book, you can also become familiar with local values by checking out open houses on weekends. Reading through the local real estate classified ads also helps you to become familiar with the local market.

The greatest risk in real estate investing is paying too much for it. You can avoid this pitfall by carefully analyzing the market before you buy. Well-informed investors know a good buy when they see one and, conversely, are fully aware if a property is overpriced.

ACQUISITION OF THE PROPER FINANCING

Another key ingredient to making a sound purchase is acquiring good financing. Good financing is critical to real estate profits because it enables you to not only earn a profit, but to also have the advantage of built-in flexible financing. On the other hand, if you involve yourself with the wrong financing, you'll face higher costs and inflexible loan terms.

Loan Assumption: The Wisest Choice

Before we describe the primary methods of creating new financing (some of which you definitely want to avoid), you should know the advantage of assuming low-interest-rate existing loans. Certain existing VA and FHA loans (originated by previous owners), and in some rare cases existing conventional loans, are fully assumable without credit qualification.

Loan assumption is far less expensive and cumbersome than is the creation of new financing under the other customary methods. Assumption of existing loans requires an assumption fee of only about $50, as opposed to the excessive loan origination fees charged by conventional lenders. (Total loan origination costs are usually 4 percent of the loan amount; thus you would have $4000 cost on a loan of $100,000.) Loan assumption also does not require the hassles of credit reports, appraisals, and employment verifications. Loan assumption, then, means no excessive loan fees, no questions, and only a small assumption fee.

Not only is loan assumption attractive from a buyer's point of view, but as a seller you have a built-in advantage because the loan you assumed as the buyer is now fully assumable when you sell. Another advantage is that you can later "wrap" this existing loan when you sell at a much higher interest rate, and make a profit on the spread in interest rates. For a full discussion of wrap-around loans, see Chapter 3.

Another advantage of loan assumption is that an assumption takes only a few days to close, not the 60 to 90 days using other methods of financing. These delays involving new loan origination are very frustrating to investors; they can easily be overcome with the ease, simplicity, and increased profitability of loan assumption.

A LARGE EQUITY POSITION

The third key ingredient to profitable realty investing is for the seller to have a large equity position in the property. A large amount of equity presents a twofold profit opportunity for the smart investor. The opportunity is twofold because if the seller is willing to carry back a note for a portion of the equity the buyer has

1). created financing which is usually at below-market cost, and

2). can subsequently be assumed or wrapped at a higher interest rate when the property is resold.

Here's how it works. Let's say you buy a house for $75,000 with a $5000 down payment. You assume the existing 8 percent loan of $40,000 and the seller carries back a note for his $30,000 equity in the property at 9 percent interest. Now you have built-in financing which another buyer can assume; or even better, you can wrap this assumable financing at a higher interest rate and make a profit on the spread in interest rates. (See Chapter 3 for more information on the wrap-around mortgage.)

Additionally, a large equity position in the property can often lead to a bargain price. Let's say that you locate a property you feel is worth $90,000 (which happens to be its listed price). The seller owes $40,000, which means a $50,000 equity position. The seller bought this property eight years ago for $50,000, and because of appreciation and paying down the loan, he or she now has a sizable gain. It is likely the seller might accept an offer of $80,000 because he or she will realize a $30,000 gain. On the other hand, if the property doesn't have a sizable amount of equity, there is little room for price negotiation.

For example, take a situation where an owner has a $40,000 first loan and a $40,000 second loan on the property. Thus, he or she owes $80,000. This owner has to sell for at least $86,000 just to cover the cost of the loans and the selling costs. Therefore, without a large equity position, there is no room for price concessions.

A MOTIVATED SELLER

The fourth ingredient of a good buy is to purchase from a motivated seller. Who is a motivated seller? A motivated seller (sometimes called a "don't wanter") is someone who, because of certain circumstances, is prepared to sell below market value. Such circumstances might be divorce, death in the family, job relocation, vacant rental and associated landlord headaches, lack of money, another property bought and ready to occupy. Any combination of these factors can contribute to motivation to sell.

The greatest-motivated sellers are those with such a combination. In these situations, the seller could be ready to look at just about any offer.

THE MORE LAND, THE BETTER

Improvements on land have value, but these improvements eventually wear down and become obsolete. It's the land, by itself, that endures and appreciates, and as time passes it emerges as the investor's most valuable asset.

Before there was anything else, there was land. It has, and always has had, certain value characteristics unlike anything else. Land has supreme value because unlike anything else, it cannot be increased in quantity. Land is required for the production of food and commodities, and provides the location for its occupants' shelter. Land provides natural resources, such as oil and mineral products; these products have value themselves.

Each plot of land is absolutely different from every other plot of land. Each plot has its own soil quality and underlying composition, its own water supply and drainage ability, its own vegetation and terrain, and its own view. With the exception of "acts of God," land by itself, unlike the improvements built upon it, cannot be increased in quantity. From feudal lords of the distant past to homeowners and developers of today, a measure of one's wealth has been described primarily as the amount of land one owns. Therefore, holding title to land is something precious indeed.

In Las Vegas a few years ago, I discovered that the best bargains were to be found in investing in homes on large parcels of land. In particular, I began specializing in the purchase of middle-class homes on half-acre lots.

The reason for this specialization was that I could get more for my money, in particular, more land; and that the sellers of these "half-acre mini-estates" never really had an accurate appraisal of the land's value. In other words, frequently you could buy a 1600-square-foot home on a half acre for about the price of a similar tract home on one-fourth the amount of land.

You see, it's often difficult to find a bargain among tract homes and condominiums because they are all so much alike. Therefore, these properties are easy to appraise. Everyone involved with the tract knows the value because all the properties are about the same. On the other hand, a half-acre mini-estate is unique. Most uninformed owners of these properties tend to give insufficient value to the land, and therein lies the opportunity for the wise investor.

Lack of sufficient land also inhibits the growth of a property. Many potential homeowners want more land so they can later add on to the house. Obviously, if there isn't enough land, expansion of the house will be limited. But more importantly, the more land you have, the better off you'll be when it comes time to convert the house to a higher use. For instance, if your home can eventually be converted to a commercial use, you'll be better off. If the land area isn't big enough, the amount of new office space you develop (not to mention its required parking area) will be limited to the small space you have available.

To make a long story short, always try to acquire as much land as you can. Over the long term, the primary value of the entire property will eventually be in the land itself.

GOOD LOCATION IN A THRIVING MARKET

The final ingredient to making a sound investment is a good location in a thriving real estate market. Much has been said over the years about the prime importance of location in real estate purchasing. This is most certainly true when buying a home for yourself, but it is not always the case when buying investment property.

Bear in mind your objective when purchasing investment

property. You want a money-maker: a property that appreciates, offers tax shelter benefits, and a better-than-average return on invested capital. The property in which you're interested may not be in the best part of town, but if it's a money-maker don't let the location stop you from making a sound *investment*. In other words, just because you wouldn't live there yourself, don't let the location stand in your way.

Instead of what to look for in a location, sometimes it's better to be aware of what to avoid. Beware of buying property in a neighborhood that has certain nuisances. This may detract from the property's value. Here are certain inquiries you should make before buying residential property:

- Is it located next to commercial buildings, such as a warehouse or factory?
- Is it adjacent to a cemetery or an undertaker?
- Is it next to a school playground where noisy children may interfere with the quiet enjoyment of the premises?
- Is it near an airport, or under the flight path of incoming or departing aircraft?
- Is the property subject to floods?
- Is there an unusual volume of nearby vehicular traffic that may prove to be a nuisance?

These are things in a location that detract from the value of residential property. You can avoid these nuisances by carefully checking out the surrounding neighborhood before commiting yourself to a long-term real estate investment.

Finally, you have to be sure you're investing in a thriving real estate market. Generally, a thriving market is considered one that is not declining in population, employment, and property values. A non-thriving market, or declining area, could be the city of Houston during the late 1980s. It was during this time that Houston experienced what economists call a "rolling recession." A glut of petroleum supplies on the world market caused oil prices to fall drastically. This resulted in oil companies cutting back on employment, with many related businesses failing. Many banks also failed during this time, partially due to real estate loans on which many unemployed people could no longer make payments. The final result was an oversupply of new housing, which most people couldn't afford to buy, and foreclosures. Eventually, the value of housing in Houston dropped dramatically because of this rolling recession.

Caution should also be taken when investing in smaller urban areas that are primarily dependent on one type of industry. If that particular industry experiences bad economic times or has to close, it's likely that the surrounding area will become depressed. On the other hand, areas that have diverse industries, such as Los Angeles or Boston, are not dependent on any one industry. These urban areas will thrive, even if one major industry fails.

Now that you have a grasp of investment objectives and the key ingredients to profitable opportunities, let's look at some profitable investment strategies.

5 PROFITABLE STRATEGIES FEATURING BUY-OPTION

After buying a property and renovating it into a habitable condition, you have several alternative ways of proceeding in order to make it a profitable money-making investment. They are: renting it with a Buy-Option, selling it on installment, selling it outright, or simply renting it. Once you've looked over the available options, you can direct your energy to the strategy that will best suit your needs, abilities, and long-term goals.

Although short-term speculation and sale of the property for all cash will be discussed, long-term investment in real estate is emphasized in this book. Granted, big profits can be realized during the short term; however, to get the most from your realty investments it's essential to think of the long term. Long-term holding periods take advantage of the effects of inflation and taxes. They also spread the high cost of buying and selling (which often are excessive over the short term) over a longer period. Good realty investments are hard to find. If you find one, negotiate its purchase, renovate it, and then sell it for all cash, you then have to find another property in which to invest the proceeds. Why not hold the investment over the long term and continue to earn profits on it? Eventually, as it appreciates in value, it can be the foundation for investment in numerous other properties.

As long as you're patient and you make use of the guidelines presented, your chances of success at real estate investment are extremely high.

BUY-OPTION; THE REAL MONEY-MAKER

Instead of simply renting out your property, consider earning $200 or more per month in cash flow by offering your tenants an option to buy it. The Buy-Option technique offers several other advantages over renting, but before we discuss them, this innovative strategy must be defined and understood.

Buy-Option is a rental agreement in which the tenant has a leasehold interest in the property, with an option to purchase it. The option to purchase is a separate part of the rental agreement. In this part, the price and terms of the Buy-Option agreement are specified. Under a typical Buy-Option contract the owner (optionor) of a property gives the tenant (optionee) the option to purchase the rented property at a specified price, within a set period of time, and for an option fee (consideration).

The consideration is paid by the tenant in installments (a portion of the rent) which are applied toward the established purchase price. For instance, let's say you could rent a house to a tenant for $700 monthly. But instead of simply renting it, you offer the tenant a Buy-Option and the tenant pays you $200 a month in option fees in addition to the monthly rent. Now, instead of collecting merely $700 monthly, you collect $900.

Buy-Option Advantages

Other than being extremely more profitable than renting, the Buy-Option has a number of other advantages:

- It's a great marketing tool. That's because you have a broad market of potential buyers who earn adequate incomes, yet they don't have adequate down payments to finance a purchase under conventional terms. Under the Buy-Option strategy, the option fee, which is paid on installment, is applied toward the purchase price. The option fee acts as the down payment, or a portion of it.
- Buy-Option tenants take better care of the occupied property than tenants who are only renting it. They tend

to make improvements to the property because of the possibility that they may eventually own it.

- Should the holder of the Buy-Option fail to exercise the option during the term of agreement, he or she forfeits all option fees already paid.
- You save a sales commission when the option is exercised. On a $100,000 sale, that's a savings of $6000.
- You benefit from earning a profit on existing underlying low-interest-rate financing because you can wrap the existing loans with a higher overriding rate of interest and make a profit on the differential.
- The buyer benefits from not having to pay loan origination fees, appraisal, or credit report. More importantly, the buyer benefits by not being required to make a large down payment. The down payment is accumulated on installment through the option fees.
- Buy-Option is safe and secure. When the option is exercised, the entire transaction is handled through a neutral trust, such as a title company. The buyer makes one payment into the trust, while the trust disburses all funds to the underlying loans, pays the taxes and insurance, and distributes the rest to the seller. In this way both buyer and seller are protected. Both can rest assured that all encumbrances are being paid.

More on the Buy-Option

Buy-Option is not an entirely new concept. In fact, owners of real property have been optioning their property for ages, but the use of options on *residential* property is relatively new. The use of an option, by itself and without a lease, is very useful to raw land speculators. For example, a knowledgeable land speculator with inside information on future land use could tie up a large land parcel with an option to buy, then sell the option at a later date to a developer.

Let's say that our knowledgeable speculator has inside information on the construction of a major thoroughfare or freeway. He or she could obtain an option on adjacent freeway land, instead of purchasing a large parcel of undeveloped land from an uninformed owner at a bargain price; later he or she could sell the option at a substantial profit to a developer, once the construction of the freeway commences.

I stumbled upon the Buy-Option concept out of pure necessity. (As has been said, "necessity is the mother of invention.") A property I own in Las Vegas was experiencing more tenant turnover than I could reasonably tolerate. So I experimented with the property during a vacancy and proceeded to run an ad in the paper offering "Rent with a Buy-Option."

The results from the Buy-Option advertisement were overwhelming. I must have received 10 times the calls I normally would have gotten under a "rental only" situation. Within a week I had a qualified Buy-Option tenant residing in the property at a monthly rate $225 higher than the old rental rate.

As time passed, I discovered all the other wonderful benefits the Buy-Option method has over renting. Besides the additional income, I noted that my Buy-Option tenants took better care of the property than did the renters. Additionally, the benefits of those great low-interest assumable loans now came into play, because the built-in financing enabled me to wrap all the existing loans with a higher overriding interest rate and make a profit on the differential. (For more details on assumable loans and the wrap-around mortgage, see Chapter 3.)

Buy-Option Example

The following is an example of a Buy-Option that I arranged several years ago in Las Vegas:

Purchase price		$88,000
Down payment	$15,000	
Assumed first loan @ 8%	40,000	
New second loan @ 9%	33,000	
Cost to renovate	1,200	

I bought this house for $88,000. It had about 2200 square feet of living space with three bedrooms and 2.5 baths, and it was located on a half acre with a breathtaking view of the Las Vegas strip. I spent about $1200 laying down solid oak floors in the living room while paneling entry walls with stained oak. The finishing touches were solid oak moldings at the entrance to the formal dining and kitchen areas.

Once the renovations were completed, I placed an advertisement in the local paper in search of my Buy-Option tenant. Here's what the ad looked like:

Rent with BUY-OPTION. 3 br, 2.5 ba, beautiful custom home on half acre, horse-zoned near Warm Springs and Valley View, fireplace, country kitchen with all appliances, oak floors, great view of strip, fenced and landscaped, fruit trees and covered patio. $1100, of which $225 applies to purchase. Call 555–3953.

Terms of this particular agreement were as follows: Tenant to have option to purchase at a price of $115,000 for one year. Down payment of $5000, of which $2700 is prepaid option fees plus $2300 cash. Balance to be financed with an all-inclusive trust deed (same as a wrap-around mortgage) at 11.5 percent for 20 years.

Within two weeks I had a qualified tenant who couldn't wait to move in. He agreed to all my terms. Here's how the numbers worked:

First loan of $40,000 payable	
@ $400 per month at 8%	$400
Second loan of $33,000 payable	
@ $420 per month at 9%	420
Taxes & insurance payable	
@ $90 per month	90
Total monthly expenses	$910

Since my Buy-Option tenant paid $1100 per month, my cash flow was $190 monthly. (If I were to simply rent this property, I would barely be able to break even at about $900 per month rent, which was the market rent for similar properties in the Las Vegas area.)

Now let's take a look at the net income from this transaction:

Monthly income	$1,100
Less: Total expenses	910
Monthly cash flow	190
Plus: Equity buildup of $310 monthly as both loans pay down	310
Net monthly cash flow and equity buildup	500
Net annual cash flow and equity buildup ($500 × 12)	$6,000

Now we can calculate return on investment (yield). Return on investment is the total investment (down payment plus renovation costs) divided into net annual income. In this case, I invested $15,000 in the down payment and spent $1200 renovating the property. (Closing costs are ignored for simplicity.) Therefore:

$$\frac{\text{Net annual income of \$6,000}}{\text{Total investment of \$16,200}} = \text{Return on investment}$$

$$\text{Return on investment} = 37.04\%$$

Return on investment is 37.04 percent, based on the period of time before the tenant exercises the option to purchase. Now let's look at what happens when the tenant exercises the option to purchase:

Option price	$115,000
Less: option fees and $2300 cash	5,000
Balance to be financed by 11.5% wrap for 20 years	110,000

Payment on $110,000 at 11.5 percent for 20 years is $1173 monthly made to the seller. (The $90 for taxes and insurance will be paid elsewhere.) Now we can examine the results after the option is exercised:

Monthly payments of principal and interest on $110,000	$1,173
The following items are what the seller continues to pay on:	

Existing first loan	$ 400
Existing second loan	420
Total seller payment	820
Cash flow to seller	353
Plus equity build-up of $310 as the existing loans pay down	310
Net monthly income	663
Net annual income before taxes	$7,956

The seller will net $663 per month ($7956 annually) on the initial $15,000 investment plus $1200 in renovation costs, for a total investment of $16,200. Now we can determine return on investment after the option is exercised, as follows:

Net annual income is divided by the total investment which results in the yield, or return on investment. Thus, $7956 is divided by $16,200 resulting in a 49.11 percent return on investment. However, we must take this one step further because the seller received a cash payment of $2300. This amount reduces the total investment to $13,900. Therefore, if we divide this amount into annual net income of $7956, the result is a 57.24 percent return on investment.

This is a phenomenal return on investment. Many shrewd, conservative investors are content with a 12 percent return on invested money. Yet this return of 57.24 percent increases to an even greater figure, year after year, because the existing underlying loans pay down more each year. This results in a greater equity build-up than the $310 given in this example. Furthermore, the seller benefits even more in 10 years. That's because after this period the existing underlying loan of $33,000 will be completely paid off. Then the seller will earn an additional $420 per month because loan payments on it will no longer be required.

The Buy-Option method offers the investor a tremendous return on investment. But *why* is it so profitable? The primary reason is that low-interest-rate loans are wrapped by a substantially higher-rate loan. In our example, we wrapped 8 and 9 percent loans at 11.5 percent. Another reason is that the property was sold for $27,000 more than what was paid for it ($115,000 versus $88,000). And a third reason is that when the option to purchase was exercised, the seller received $2300 cash, which substantially reduced the total investment.

As you can see, the Buy-Option method can be a very lucrative tool in real estate investment. Buy-Option works. It has broad market appeal because many potential home buyers like the idea of making their down payment on the installment plan (paying option fees which apply toward the purchase of the home). You'd be surprised at how many potential home buyers there are who earn enough income to afford to buy a home, yet they don't have an adequate down payment to purchase it under other methods of financing. The option buyer also benefits by not having to pay loan origination fees.

As a review, Figure 5.1 is a simplified illustration of the mechanics of the Buy-Option using the same numbers from the earlier examples.

From the illustration given in Figure 5.1, the seller continues to pay only $820 per month on existing loans. Taxes and insurance of $90 are now paid by the buyer. The buyer pays the seller $1173 per month on the new wrap-around mortgage at 11.5 percent for 20 years. The differential in monthly payments is $353 ($1173 − $820), which represents the cash flow to the seller. When you add equity build-up of $310, the result is $663 in net income per month before income taxes.

Figure 5.2 is a sample Buy-Option agreement. Please note that it is kept separate from the rental agreement, just to make things less complicated.

Put Everything in Writing

The exact terms of the option must be spelled out in the Buy-Option agreement. This way there will be no doubts or need for further negotiation. Both the buyer and seller will know exactly *whose* responsibility it is to do *what*, and for *how much*.

An option to purchase can be as creative as the buyer and seller want it to be; however, it should be kept relatively simple to avoid any misunderstandings. Should you decide to give the tenant a longer term on the option (more than one year), you then essentially have two methods of determining

The following is a simplified illustration of the mechanics of the buy-option:

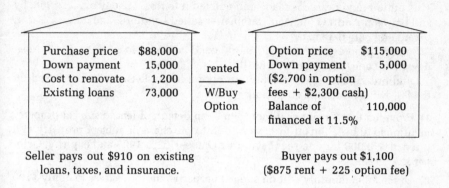

Seller pays out $910 on existing
loans, taxes, and insurance.

Buyer pays out $1,100
($875 rent + 225 option fee)

The following is what occurs when the Buy-Option tenant exercises the option to buy:

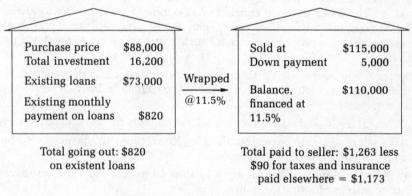

Total going out: $820
on existent loans

Total paid to seller: $1,263 less
$90 for taxes and insurance
paid elsewhere = $1,173

Figure 5.1 Buy-Option Example

the selling price over the extended period. After the first year, you could set the option price at the existing price plus 1.5 times the Consumer Price Index (CPI). The other alternative is to arbitrarily fix a selling price at which the tenant can buy the property during a specific term, such as $100,000 after one year, $110,000 after two years, and $120,000 after three years. (I personally prefer using 1.5 times the CPI because real estate values historically tend to increase at about 1.5 times the rate of inflation, to which the CPI relates.)

Figure 5.2 Example of a Buy-Option Agreement

This option to purchase is made and entered into this ____day of ____1988, by and between Andrew McLean, hereinafter called Landlord, and _____, hereinafter called Tenant.

Subject property is a single story condominium located at 6182 Meadowgrass Lane, Las Vegas, NV, 89103.

Landlord hereby agrees to grant an option to purchase to Tenant based on the following terms and conditions:

1) Provided that Tenant shall not then be in default of leased subject property mentioned above, Tenant to have option to purchase of subject property at a price of $70,000 for one year beginning October ____, 1988 and expiring October ____, 1989.

2) Of the $695 monthly rent on subject property landlord agrees to apply $100 of it towards the purchase price. This $100 is referred to as the option fee.

3) Subject property will be financed by an all-inclusive trust deed payable at 10.75 percent interest in favor of the landlord for a term of twenty (20) years. Said AITD is in the amount of $67,500, payable at $685.28 monthly.

4) Tenant agrees to pay a total of $2,500 down at time of execution of this option. The down payment consists of 12 option fee payments of $100 each, $1000 cash, and the landlord agrees to apply the $300 security deposit to the balance owing. Landlord agrees that Tenant may apply more to the down payment.

5) Tenant agrees to pay all taxes, insurance, and mortgage payments into a trust account for disbursement to all parties concerned and pay for such a trust account.

6) Tenant further agrees to purchase subject property in "as-is" condition.

7) Landlord agrees to have all underlying loans, taxes, and insurance current at time of execution of this agreement.

8) Both Landlord and Tenant agree to split all normal closing costs, except Tenant is to pay for title insurance.

The parties hereto have executed this option on this date first above written:
By _____Landlord   By _____Tenant

Structuring the Option Agreement

For clarity, certain items should be specifically spelled out in the option agreement. Both the prepaid cleaning and security deposits can be applied toward the down payment as part of the agreement. If appliances are to be included in the selling price, say so in the agreement; otherwise spell out the price you require for such items individually.

Another consideration is what rate of interest to charge the buyer on the wrap-around mortgage. It makes good business sense to be fair and reasonable. Bear in mind that you will be competing with conventional lenders, because you are, in effect, acting as a conventional lender when you wrap existing loans (you're actually creating a new loan). Therefore, charge a rate of interest comparable to what conventional lenders are charging. But remember, you do not charge loan origination fees! This means substantial savings to the prospective buyer. This is an important selling feature that deserves further attention.

Conventional lenders have a variety of incidental charges that are added to the cost of originating a new loan, including the credit report at about $75, appraisal at about $150, 1 to 2 percent of the loan proceeds in points, plus the inconvenience and time necessary to complete the required paperwork. With this in mind, remind your potential buyers of the convenience and cost-saving benefits they receive under the Buy-Option. Also tell them about the safety and security of this method (discussed earlier in this chapter).

Three Important Notes about Buy-Option

1). In a Buy-Option agreement it is important that you state the following: "The rent is [a specified amount], of which [a specified amount] applies as the monthly option fee." Spell out that the rent is, let's say, $900 per month of which $200 applies toward the purchase price. This is better than saying "the rent is $700 and the option fee is $200," because if the tenant decides not to pay the option fee, he or she is only required to pay rent of $700.

2). Don't forget that in order for the Buy-Option method to be used, the existing underlying loans need to be fully assumable. This means that for those loans to be wrapped with a new all-inclusive loan, they must not have a due-on-sale clause.

3). As part of your "tools of the trade," buy a book that calculates interest rates and associated monthly loan payments, such as *Payment Tables For Monthly Mortgage Loans*, published by Contemporary Books. These and other similar books, are available in most bookstores.

SELLING ON INSTALLMENT

Instead of renting or optioning your property to a tenant, you could sell it on installment. This method would be more appropriate and profitable if you have underlying low-interest-rate assumable financing already built in. Let's say, for example, you purchase a property with an existing 8 percent first loan and the seller carries back a second at 9 percent. You could resell the property and allow the buyer to assume all this built-in financing; but why not make a profit on the built-in financing and sell on installment?

If you sell the property outright, you're totally cashed out; you now have to find a place in which to invest the proceeds realized from the sale. On the other hand, you can earn a substantial profit by wrapping the existing financing with a new loan for 20 or 30 years.

Now let's look at how much you'd gain by selling a property on installment with a wrap, as opposed to selling it by carrying back a second loan while allowing the buyer to assume the existing first loan.

Here are the details: The selling price is $100,000; the existing first loan is at 8 percent with a balance owing of $46,000; 22 years remain until payoff.

If you sell this property on installment for $100,000, the following is what would occur: The buyer puts $10,000 down, while the balance of $90,000 is wrapped at 11 percent for 30 years. This results in a monthly payment of $857 for 30 years. The accumulated monthly payments total $308,520.

Another alternative would be to accept a $10,000 down payment and carry back a second loan at 11 percent for 30 years.

CARRYING BACK A SECOND LOAN

Using this method, you allow the buyer to assume the existing first loan of $46,000 and carry back a second loan of $44,000. Here's how the numbers work:

Payment on $46,000 first loan for 22 years $367
Payment on $44,000 new second loan for
   30 years   419
Total accumulated payments over entire
   terms for both loans $247,728
Compared to a wrap at 11% payable at
   $857 monthly for 30 years $308,520
The difference is $60,792

As you can see, you gain $60,792 by selling on installment with a wrap, as opposed to carrying back a second loan and allowing the buyer to assume your valuable, low-interest, first loan.

Existing low-interest-rate financing is a valuable asset. Try to maintain it as long as you can. And always attempt to wrap these valuable loans with higher wrap-around loans. The results will be very rewarding, as you can earn substantially more in margin of profitability.

SELLING OUTRIGHT

Selling outright, or being totally cashed out of the property, essentially has only one advantage and several glaring disadvantages. The one advantage is that you immediately realize the profit after the sale, which means you'll have plenty of ready cash available. But this is only an advantage if you have a good place in which to reinvest the proceeds.

If you plan on adhering to the long-term investment theory, you must envision your real estate investments as tiny seedlings planted throughout a sprawling orchard. While you feed and water the seedlings, you continue to plant new ones. In reality, your seedlings are individual investment properties throughout the city (the orchard); you nurture them through renovation (giving new life), and in turn these seedlings grow to be giant redwoods. In the process, and in return for all the loving care you've given them, they pay you back with generous amounts of appreciation (not to mention tax-free income).

Now consider the disadvantages of being cashed out of the property through an outright sale. The most undesirable aspect of such a sale is that now you have to find another investment for the proceeds from the sale. You could put the money in savings, but who wants to earn a meager 5 percent? Another alternative is to invest in stocks or bonds, but then you need sound investment advice to prosper in historically turbulent markets. Realistically, you have to seek out a new real estate money-maker which can earn more than a thin 5 percent.

The other glaring disadvantage of being cashed out is that, under certain conditions, income taxes have to be paid on the gain from the sale. (Income taxes can be deferred if within a year of the sale another property of greater value is purchased.)

Let's face it: An outright sale eliminates property accumulation and makes ready cash available for frivolous spending. New cars, boats, and vacations are nice, but hardly a wise investment for someone who wants to be financially independent by the age of 40.

These are good reasons for not selling the property, and these reasons apply most of the time; but sometimes they don't, and those are the times when you *should* sell the property.

For example, you need the cash to better your investment position, so you decide to sell. The next property you want is a real bargain; the price is right, the terms are great, but you don't have the down payment. For any number of reasons you're against taking out a loan or taking a partner with cash. Under these circumstances, you might consider selling one of your properties to raise the necessary down payment, especially if it improves your financial condition. Let's assume that you could sell one of your properties in which you have a large equity position. The property you want is a 20-unit apartment building, and the owner requires $30,000 down. You decide that by selling the property and buying the apartment building, you'll substantially increase your cash flow and leverage. You then will have definitely improved your financial condition.

RENTING

Bear in mind that real estate is essentially a long-term investment. Properties you buy today, especially with a small down
payment, will probably not be highly profitable in the beginning. But as time goes on, your costs remain relatively fixed
while rents and values gradually rise. This means that a property on which you initially break even will, after a few years,
show a substantial net income and greater value. As an example, let's say you buy a house with a small down payment
and rent it out for $700 per month. Your total expenses on the
house are also $700 per month which, except for equity build-
up, is a break-even situation. It is likely that one year later you
could rent the same property for $800 per month, allowing
you $100 per month in net profit.

In a similar situation, let's say that you had a second loan
on the property that would be paid off after eight years. Once
it's paid off, you're that much further ahead in net income because you no longer have to pay on the second loan. But more
importantly, the second loan was paid off with money you derived from your tenants.

If your decision is to rent the property, you have to decide
on either a long-term lease or on a month-to-month rental
agreement. First consider the pros and cons of each. The long-
term lease (one year or more) has one set of primary advantages: securing the tenant over a long term, essentially limiting
turnover, and assuring a fairly stable flow of income over the
term of the lease. (I say "fairly stable" because in reality you
cannot guarantee that a long-term tenant won't move out without regard to lease obligations and/or before its expiration.)

There are two primary disadvantages to a long-term lease.
The first is that you've restricted the saleability of the property, since the lease would take priority over occupation rights
should the property be sold before the lease expires. (The
lease and all rights belonging to it are conveyed if the property
is sold.) The second disadvantage is that under a long-term
lease agreement, you're restricted in the amount of rent you
can charge by the terms of the lease.

Under a month-to-month rental agreement, the only real disadvantage is that your tenant is obligated only to occupy and pay rent in monthly increments. The advantages are that under such a short-term rental agreement you don't limit the saleability of the property, and you're entitled to increase the rent after 30 days.

In conclusion, simple renting out your property is a proven method of realizing a reasonable yield on your investment. However, the Buy-Option method outperforms rentals, not only economically, but also through fewer hassles. If you concentrate your efforts on maintaining Buy-Option investments, not only will you earn a higher return on investment, you'll achieve your goal of retiring "on the house" that much sooner.

CONVERTING AN UNDER-RENTED BUILDING INTO A MONEY-MAKER

Another profitable strategy is to buy an under-rented building and raise the rents, thereby increasing cash flow and property value.

Income property is evaluated by the income it earns. If you can locate an under-rented income property and substantially increase the income, you'll not only earn more income, you'll also substantially increase the property's value.

Take, for example, a four-unit building containing four two-bedroom units renting at $400 monthly. You know that similar two-bedroom apartments in the area rent for $500 monthly. Let's see how much in additional income and property value you'll gain by buying this property at its current market value, then increasing the rents $100 per unit.

Current gross income at $400 rent	$19,200
Less: Annual expenses at 40%	7,680
Equals: Net operating income of	11,520

Based on a 10 percent capatalization rate, this property is valued at $115,200. Now, if we increase the rents by $100 per unit, let's see what happens:

Projected gross income at $500 rent	$24,000
Less: Annual expenses at 40%	9,600
Equals: Net operating income of	14,400

Based on a 10 percent capitalization rate, this property's projected value is $144,000, and the property's income has increased by $2880. More importantly, the property's value has increased by $28,800. (A more detailed description of evaluation of income property is offered in Chapter 6.)

Under-rented properties can be found almost anywhere. Landlords, especially absentee ones, tend to leave things as they are. They don't like to raise rents, and tend to allow tenants to remain in the property at below-market rents over extended periods. In fact, many of these landlords are unaware of the prevailing market rents in the area. This is why the shrewd and informed investor can make a nice profit by investing in an under-rented income property.

FIXING UP YOUR PROPERTY

A question you'll probably ask yourself is whether to do the repairs yourself, or to hire the job out every time you buy a fixer-upper. That decision depends on how handy you are and whether you have adequate fix-up money to pay for professional labor. If you have plenty of cash and can't spare the time to do it yourself, then I would suggest hiring the work out. But if you're like most of us, always scraping for a buck and wanting to earn some "sweat equity," then you'd be wise to do most of the work (within your capabilities) yourself.

Personally, I enjoy cosmetic work—painting and wallpapering, and sometimes laying down a beautiful hardwood floor. When I do hire the work out, I make a point of watching what's being done and asking plenty of questions; next time, I might be capable of doing the job myself.

Hiring a Contractor

If you decide to hire a contractor, follow these guidelines:

- Discuss the job you want done with at least two contractors and get written bids for the work.
- Talk to your neighbors. Ask them if they can recommend someone. Good craftspeople build their business on their reputations. Satisfied customers will be your best guide to reputable contractors.
- Get at least three references per contractor and check them out. Call each one and ask whether there were any problems, and if so, whether they were corrected. Find out if there were any extra charges and whether the work was completed on time.

Doing it Yourself

Remember that the best fix-up properties are those that simply need some cleaning and cosmetic work inside and out. Avoid getting involved with extremely old klunkers that require a new roof, new plumbing, or new concrete. These are problem areas that usually require a specialized contractor and plenty of cash. Unless you can do some of this special work yourself, stick with properties that require only minor cosmetic work: those that just need some tastefully appointed painting and wallpapering, and perhaps a new carpet.

Painting the Interior. Use latex paints for the interior, because they're easy to apply, can be thinned and cleaned up with water, dry quickly, and have little or no odor. Flat latex is best for interior walls and ceilings. Semi-gloss or enamel finishes are better on doors, window trim, baseboards, and bathroom and kitchen walls. The semi-gloss or enamel finish will tolerate more scrubbing and abuse than will flat paints.

An off-white color like antique white, beige, or light tan is best. Be careful with dark colors. They tend to make rooms appear smaller. Choose a neutral color which will go with different colors of furniture, and one that appeals to most people's tastes. Bright red, pink. purple, or dark green are likely to clash with most furniture colors.

You want the finished product to be color-coordinated and in good taste.

If you keep all your rentals painted in a standard color, you'll work more efficiently, avoiding partly-filled paint cans of a variety of colors. Light colors make a room appear larger than dark colors, fit nicely with most furniture schemes, and look clean.

Careless painting wastes time and can be a really messy experience. Proper surface preparation is necessary.

Before going ahead with surface preparation, make sure you have all your paint supplies (on which, by the way, you can save money by purchasing five-gallon cans of paint instead of single gallons). Next, wash the walls and woodwork with soap and water. (Paint adheres better to a clean, non-glossy finish.) Fill all cracks and holes with spackling. Let them dry and sand them down. Remove all fixtures, electrical plates, and switch covers from surfaces to be painted; cover everything with dropcloths to protect the furniture and the floor. Then apply paint to the ceiling first, then the walls; finish up with the trim and semi-gloss work.

Landscaping. In most cases, fix-up properties will require you to dress up the exterior grounds—particularly the front of the house—to make it more appealing. Keep in mind that first impressions are lasting ones. If a prospective tenant or buyer drives up to inspect your property and the grounds are shabby, the prospect is likely to just keep driving. However, if your lawn is well-maintained and tidy, the property will definitely deserve further attention and inspection from a prospective buyer or tenant.

Carpeting. When you're dealing with fixer-uppers, nine times out of 10 it will be necessary to replace the carpet after buying the property. When it's time to consider the purchase of new carpeting, first do some shopping around to get a good price. The carpeting industry is highly competitive, and you will find a large number of suppliers from which to choose.

Wall-to-wall carpeting, especially if it's new, of good quality, and in good taste, will give your units a special glow of warmth and luxury. Stay with light colors, such as "earth tones" of tan and beige. A light gray is also very nice, and suits almost any furniture decor.

6 HOW TO EVALUATE A SPECIFIC PROPERTY

There are a number of proven methods of appraising real estate, but we will concern ourselves with two of them. They are the capitalization (income) approach and the comparable sale method. Generally speaking, the capitalization method analyzes income and expenses to arrive at an appraised value, while the comparable sales approach compares the subject property to similar properties which recently sold.

APPRAISAL BY CAPITALIZATION

Any kind of income property can accurately be evaluated using the capitalization method of appraisal. This includes single-family homes, but only when income can be derived from the property.

Figure 6.1 is a simplified operating statement with which we can begin our analysis of a specific property. Later on in this chapter, we will look at a more detailed operating statement on the same property. From the operating statement, we can determine both the return on investment and its value.

Now let's take a closer look at each item. Item 1 is the gross annual rental income. This is the total yearly rent the property would earn at 100 percent occupancy. In this example, the property is a duplex with each unit renting at $500 per month. Therefore, the gross annual income is $500 × 2 × 12 months, equaling $12,000.

Item 2 is the sum of all operating expenses before loan pay-

Description of property: A duplex including 2-1 bedroom units each renting at $500 per month.

1. Gross annual income		$12,000
2. Less operating expenses	4,800	
3. Net operating income	7,200	
4. Less mortgage interest payments	5,400	
5. Equals gross equity income	1,800	
6. Less depreciation allowance	2,085	
7. Equals taxable income (loss)	($285)	

Figure 6.1 Simplified Operating Statement

ments. These include an allowance for vacancy and credit losses, property taxes, insurance, advertising, supplies, repairs, and maintenance.

Item 3 is the net operating income (NOI), the result of deducting total operating expenses from gross rental income. This figure represents what the property would earn if purchased for cash, free and clear of any loans. It is also used to determine a capitalized value by dividing a suitable cap rate into the NOI. (A more detailed explanation of capitalization will be discussed later in this chapter.)

Item 4 represents the interest portion of the loan payment(s). The principal portion is not included because it is considered equity income.

Item 5 is the gross equity income. It is the result of deducting the interest portion of the loan payments from the NOI. It is the actual pre-tax cash flow and principal buildup earned by the property.

Item 6 is the depreciation allowance. In this case $2085 can be deducted from gross equity income for 27.5 years. Depreciation is the tax shelter benefit of owning income-producing real estate. Note that in this example gross equity income is $1800; yet because of depreciation, this property actually shows an after-tax *loss* of $285. To amplify, the property is earning $1800 annually, but because of depreciation benefits, it shows an after-tax loss of $285 which in most cases can be written off against ordinary income.

Item 7 is the taxable income, the result of deducting a depreciation allowance from gross equity income.

Determining Value by Capitalization

The rate of return upon invested capital is called "capitalization rate" or "cap rate." It is defined as the rate of return—expressed as a percentage—that's considered reasonable to expect for a certain type of investment. The capitalization method uses the net operating income (NOI) of the subject property, which is then "capitalized" to determine value.

The appraiser determines a rate of return, or cap rate, that is relevant to the going rate for that type of property. The selected cap rate is usually within a range of 8 to 14 percent. The appraiser determines the rate within this range by considering the risk of the investment along with the type of property and the quality of income.

For example, if an investor were considering investing in a high-risk area (high-crime slum area), he or she would expect a high rate of return on his investment. Thus, a cap rate of 13 or 14 percent would be selected. If the investor were to invest in an average area, a rate of 10 or 11 percent would be selected. And if the investor planned to invest in a prime area where property values show above-average appreciation and there is less risk to the investor, then a cap rate of 8 or 9 percent would be selected.

From the operating statement in figure 6.1, the NOI in item 3 is determined to be $7200. Now we can capitalize the NOI to determine its value based on different cap rates. Let's say the property is located in an average middle-class neighborhood. To determine a capitalized value you would divide the NOI of $7200 by an average rate of return of 10 percent. The result is a value of $72,000. In other words, to earn a 10 percent return on your investment, you would pay $72,000 for the property. If you expected an 11 percent return on the property, then divide the NOI of $7200 by 11 percent, which results in a projected purchase price of $65,455.

Determining Total Return on Investment

From the capitalization approach we have determined a range of values based on certain selected cap rates. From Figure 6.1, we know that the value of the property at a 10 percent cap rate is $72,000. Now, let's explore what you can expect as a total return on investment based on a purchase price of $72,000.

To analyze total return on investment we will analyze the down payment (the investment) along with gross equity income and projected appreciation. In our example (Figure 6.1), the gross equity income is $1800. To determine return in investment before appreciation, divide the down payment into gross equity income. In this case, if you buy the property for $72,000 with a $10,000 down payment, the property would earn a pre-tax gross equity income of $1800. Therefore, if you divide $1800 by the investment of $10,000, the resulting return on investment is 18 percent.

To determine total return on investment, we now have to add to our calculations how much you expect the property to appreciate annually. We have estimated that inflation will probably average about 6 percent annually. If this is so, then real estate values will (on average) appreciate one-and-a-half times the rate of inflation. Therefore you can reasonably expect the value of your real estate holdings to increase at 9 percent a year based on a 6 percent rate of inflation. (Please note that these are average figures. In certain parts of the country, especially where buildable land is scarce, the average rate of appreciation exceeds 15 percent. I am simply trying to round out an overall useful average that is generally applicable.)

Thus, if we presume that you buy the duplex in Fig. 6.1 for $72,000, you could expect a 9 percent annual rate of appreciation. Nine percent of $72,000 is $6480. Therefore, if you add $6480 to the $1800 gross equity income, the result is $8280. To determine total return on investment, simply divide $8280 by your $10,000 investment and the result is an unbelievable 82.8 percent annual total return on your investment.

Bear in mind that return on investment, by itself, without anticipated appreciation, is what you'll actually earn while owning the property. Any appreciation you earn cannot be realized until you *sell* the property. Therefore, you should base your evaluation of income property on a certain expected rate of return. Then, any amount of appreciation, no matter how great or small, will be that much value added to your overall investment.

Description: Duplex with 2 1-bedroom units renting at $500 monthly.

Gross annual rental income		$12,000
Less annual operating expenses:		
Vacancy & credit loss (5%)	600	
Property taxes	1240	
Insurance	800	
Reserve for repairs & replacement (5%)	600	
Advertising	200	
Trash removal	240	
Business license	50	
Supplies	200	
Lawn maintenance	870	
Total annual operating expenses	4,800	− 4,800
Net operating income (NOI)		7,200
Mortgage payments (interest only)		− 5,400
Gross equity income (cash flow + equity build-up)		1,800
Depreciation allowance		(2,085)
Taxable income (loss)		(285)

Figure 6.2 Detailed Operating Statement

As a general rule, I would use a 12.5 percent return (before appreciation) as a minimum return you should expect. In other words, tailor your analysis to expect nothing less than a 12.5 percent return on your investment.

Figure 6.2 is a more detailed operating statement regarding the duplex we already discussed:

A Final Note on Capitalization and Return on Investment

From Figure 6.2, we determined that based on a 10 percent cap rate the property is worth $72,000. We also determined that the return on investment is 18 percent, predicated on a $10,000 down payment. But what if during your analysis you learn that our duplex is under-rented? In other words, you know that similar properties in the neighborhood rent for $575 per month and that once you own the property you could raise the rents to $575.

Based on this new information, let's do a quick analysis to see what the property is worth and the rate of return you could expect after rents are increased. Raising the rents $75 each on the two units increases gross equity income from $1800 to $3600 ($75 × 2 × 12 = $1800). Therefore, instead of an 18 percent return on investment, by increasing the rents you have doubled your return on investment to 36 percent.

Now let's look at the capitalized value after increasing the rents. The NOI before rental increases was $7200. If we increase the annual rent $1800, then the projected NOI will be $9,000 (assuming operating expenses remain constant). If we capitalize the new NOI at 10 percent, the result is an appraised value of $90,000 (based on a 10 percent cap rate). As you can see, by increasing the rent of an under-rented building, you substantially increase its value.

APPRAISAL BY COMPARABLE SALES

The comparable sales method is the most common method of evaluating residential, non-income-producing real estate. This method compares the subject property with similar comparable properties that recently sold in the same area. The valuation of the subject property is adjusted according to certain amenities, such as quality of construction, square-footage differential, existence of a garage or pool, and individual location.

A simple application of the comparable sales method would be to compare the subject property with at least three similar properties that have recently sold, are located within the same area, and essentially have no meaningful differences. For instance, assume all three comparables sold at a price between $80,000 and $82,000, and had the same square footage and lot size. The subject property is similar in quality of construction and lot size; however, it has a 300-square-foot den and a swimming pool, amenities which the comparables do not have. Therefore, based on this information, the subject property is worth $81,000, plus the additional amenities of a den and swimming pool. You determine that at today's construction costs, a 300-square-foot den would cost $40 per square foot, for a total cost of $12,000. You also determine that a swimming

Market Analysis Form

Subject property adddress _____ Date _____

Information on similar properties in same general area that may have the same approximate value.

Currently for sale

Address	Bedrooms	Baths	Den Fam. rm	Sq. Ft.	Price/ sq. ft.	Mortgages	Interest rate	Days on market

Sold within last six months

Note: Realtors and old MLS books can be helpful for finding past sale information.

Figure 6.3 Market Analysis Form

pool would cost $10,000. So your final opinion of value would be $81,000 + $12,000 for the den + $10,00 for the pool, or an appraised value of $103,000.

The Market Analysis Form (Figure 6.3) will be helpful when you use the comparable sale method of appraisal.

7 HOW TO NEGOTIATE THE PURCHASE

You've been combing the local area seeking a good buy and you find a property that looks promising. Now what do you do? First, gather all the information you can about the property and do a financial analysis on it. Before you can make a formal written offer, you have to be adequately prepared. This brings us to an important point: Do not make verbal offers.

NEVER MAKE A VERBAL OFFER

The purchase of real property is a substantial undertaking with a great deal of money at stake. For the seller, the sale of a particular property is likely to be the largest money transaction in which he or she ever participated. You can't expect to look the seller in the eye and say, "I'm interested in buying your house, but $90,000 is too much. I'll give you $75,000." Not only have you asked the seller to reduce the price substantially, but you have also failed to clarify the remaining details of the transaction. These details include such important matters as size of a down payment, financing arrangements, and date of taking possession. It's just not practical to handle all these details face to face.

THE FORMAL WRITTEN OFFER

The correct way to negotiate the purchase of real property is to prepare a formal written offer, which, along with an earnest money deposit (amount of money showing buyer's good faith), is submitted to the seller for consideration. The written offer to purchase spells out, in detail, all the terms and conditions under which you are willing to purchase the property. It's the offer of a binding contract, which—when accepted and signed by the seller—binds you legally to its contents. This brings us to another important point. Whatever you and the seller finally agree on—in writing—you're going to have to live with. So it is absolutely imperative that you be fully informed of comparable values and that you bargain for a good deal.

Before you initiate a written offer, establish the maximum dollar amount you are willing to pay for the property. This price represents your final offer. Anything above this price is not worth paying, because then the property is no longer a bargain. The price you actually pay should be substantially below the established maximum; if it is, you've definitely made a good investment.

How Much Should You Offer?

On average, real estate sells at about 5 percent below its asking price. This doesn't mean, however, that you should make all your offers at 5 percent below list price. Five percent only represents an average, which means that some properties sell for 10 percent below asking price, while others may sell at exactly list price. Incidentally, certain properties have been known to sell *above* the listed price, especially when more than one interested party gets involved and a frenzied "bidding war" begins. Usually, the only party that benefits when two or more people are competing to buy a property is the seller. Avoid getting involved when other buyers are making offers on the same property. The additional competition makes it too difficult to get a good buy. Besides, why bother with competition when several other potential bargains are available from motivated sellers? You need only to locate them.

It is usually presumed that the seller built in to the asking price a margin of price reduction to allow for negotiation. You don't want to offer full price, unless you know that the seller is firm on his price and that the property is a very good deal—

well worth the asking price. On the other hand, a ridiculously low offer may not be taken seriously by the seller.

Your objective, then, is to make an offer that has a reasonable chance of being accepted by the seller. If it isn't accepted, at least it should be good enough to stimulate a counteroffer from the seller.

How much should you offer? From your homework, you should already have an established maximum price you would pay. Also, let's assume you know that similar homes in the area have sold at approximately the price the seller is asking for his property. Therefore, assuming that the list price is fairly close to market value, offer about 10 percent below asking price.

Bargaining to reach agreement is what negotiating is all about. Unless you're prepared to pay all cash, and at the seller's asking price, you will be bargaining for price and terms. As a general rule, if a seller is firm on price, then negotiate terms. If he is firm on terms, then negotiate price. If the seller is firm on neither, then negotiate both. If he is firm on both, then start looking for another investment (unless, of course, the asking price is just too good to pass up, which is unlikely).

Other Considerations in Making the Offer

At this point, consider what you can offer the seller in terms of a down payment. A total cash down payment is not always necessary to consummate a purchase. Personal property items, such as vehicles, boats, recreation vehicles, and appliances can often be used instead of cash. If the seller is nearing retirement age, he or she might consider a boat or RV for his or her equity in the property. Or instead of looking for cash, he or she might be looking for income, which means you could offer a secured mortgage for his or her other equity in the property.

The important thing to remember is that cash is a valuable asset; it's working capital, and without it you're out of business. And remember the principle of leverage: the less you have invested in the property, the more leverage you will have, and the greater your return on investment will be.

Counteroffers

Frequently the seller will find your initial offer unacceptable and in most cases will propose a counteroffer. Once a counteroffer is proposed, your initial offer is terminated.

The procedure of offer/counteroffer is important because it brings out the flexibility of both buyer and seller. Always remember that you should have in mind a maximum dollar amount you will pay. In the event you're confronted with an inflexible seller, don't waste any more of your time. Chalk up your time and effort to experience and find another property. If, on the other hand, the property remains an excellent buy, then continue to pursue an agreement. Quite often, especially when a good buy is at hand, a property is sold right out from under a negotiating buyer because he or she persisted in demanding excessive concessions from the seller.

CLAUSES WITHIN THE OFFER THAT PROTECT YOU

Certain contingency clauses should be written into the offer to protect you; here is a discussion of two of them.

Inspection Clause

If the property is a multi-unit rental building, it's just not practical to inspect the interior or every unit prior to buying. The seller cannot be expected to disturb every tenant within the building just to satisfy the whims of a touring prospective buyer. Therefore, the seller can exhibit a *typical* unit to a prospect, then allow him or her to examine the remaining units once a contract is agreed on.

Thus, an inspection clause should be worded in such a way that allows the buyer to inspect all units prior to closing. An example of such a clause would be: "This offer is contingent upon all rental units being in essentially the same condition as the unit already inspected."

New Loan Clause

If you're buying a property on which you intend to originate a new first mortgage, you will need a contingency clause that voids the contract in case you cannot get the loan. Therefore, make sure there's a clause similar to the following: "This offer is contingent upon buyer acquiring a new first mortgage in the approximate amount of $_____ at prevailing rates and terms within 16 working days of acceptance of this offer." Thus, if you can't acquire the new first mortgage, this contingency clause voids the offer and you get your deposit back.

Contingency clauses can cover almost anything, and you need certain ones to limit your liability. However, keep in mind that the seller or his/her agent will attempt to eliminate excessive contingencies, because they tend to complicate what would otherwise be a simple closing.

AMOUNT OF EARNEST-MONEY DEPOSIT

Any amount ranging from $500 to $3000 would be an appropriate sum for the earnest-money deposit. The recommended amount is $500, so as to limit your liability. Why? Because in the event you're forced, for whatever reason, to default on the transaction, you need to keep your losses to a minimum. Should your offer be accepted, it is likely that the seller, or the seller's agent, will require a larger deposit to secure the transaction and protect his or her interest.

8 WHERE TO FIND YOUR "DIAMOND IN THE ROUGH"

Sources of potentially good realty investments are almost boundless; you only have to know where to look for them. Nevertheless, if it were easy to locate and purchase bargain-priced real estate, everyone would be doing so. Since it is not easy, perseverance is needed to first locate and then buy the right property for you.

On average, two-thirds of all the real estate for sale is listed with realtors, but you also have a wide selection from other sources such as For Sale By Owners (FSBOs), HUD property, and other types of foreclosure property.

NEWSPAPER ADS

You'll find homes and multi-unit buildings listed in the classified section of your local newspaper under "Real Estate For Sale."

For Sale by Owners (FSBOs) will require you to deal directly with the owner. Start by circling with a pen the properties that appear interesting, then cut them out and staple the circled ads to the left-hand margin of a plain piece of paper. Now you have adequate space to make notes adjacent to the stapled-down advertisements.

For both FSBOs and realtor ads, begin phoning about the cut-out advertisements. Inquire into available financing and down payment requirements. Ask about square footage, lot size, condition of the property, and reason for selling. Get as much information as you can. Then, if the property still sounds promising, make an appointment with the owner to visit it.

WORKING WITH A REALTOR AND THE MLS

A top-notch real estate agent is a priceless asset. A competent agent looks out for your interest. He or she makes available to you properties to which you otherwise would not have access. When you locate the property that deserves an offer to buy, your agent will present the offer and will help with negotiating the final agreement between you and the seller. Once a satisfactory agreement is reached, the agent will follow the transaction through its normal channels, securing any loose ends that might otherwise jeopardize the closing.

To work effectively, the agent needs to know exactly what you're looking for; so give your agent specifics of exactly what it is you want. For instance: a fixer-upper priced below $100,000, with assumable fixed-rate financing below 10 percent, requiring a maximum down payment of $7000. These are specific parameters that act as guidelines for the agent.

An agent has access to the Multiple Listing Service (MLS), which covers every home listed for sale with a realtor in your area. It's the agent's responsibility to keep abreast of what's on the market and to look for property that's right for you.

Real estate agents who belong to the MLS have access to the MLS book, which is usually published every other week, maintaining up-to-date information on all listed properties. It is an invaluable tool for investors. Once you get to know an agent, ask him/her to lend you last week's MLS book so you can study the listings. (Technically speaking, lending out MLS books to nonmembers is against MLS rules; however, it's done all the time.)

Once you have a recent MLS book, go through it carefully while noting properties of interest. On a separate sheet of paper, note the property addresses and MLS page numbers. Then, later when you phone about, or drive by a property, you can make notes on the reference sheet. Also, important information regarding recent sale prices are usually listed in the back portion of the book; this information will help you to get a feel for values in the local market.

HUD PROPERTY

Residential property owned by the United States Department of Housing and Urban Development (HUD) are a great source of investment for anyone. These properties have previously been foreclosed on, were financed under VA and FHA loan programs, and are now owned by HUD.

HUD lists its properties for sale with licensed real estate brokers. Buyers may not submit offers directly to HUD except in circumstances where they cannot obtain the services of a licensed broker.

All HUD properties are sold as-is, without warranties. It is the buyer's responsibility to determine the condition of the property.

HUD properties can be financed with or without HUD mortgage insurance. For those properties listed "with HUD insurance," the buyer may seek an FHA-insured loan from a private lender and use the mortgage proceeds to buy the house from HUD. For properties listed "without HUD insurance," the terms are all cash to HUD in 30 days, with no contingencies for financing.

Certain real estate brokers specialize in HUD property. If you want to inspect a particular HUD property, a HUD master key and lock box key can be obtained from any of the area management brokers. They usually advertise numerous HUD offerings in the Real Estate For Sale section in your local newspaper.

The listing price of each property is HUD's estimate of fair market value. However, HUD will accept offers for less than the listing price.

Investing in HUD property can be a very rewarding experience; however, you should be aware of certain shortcomings. You have to remember that you're dealing with the federal government, which means lots of bureaucratic red tape. HUD requires all kinds of special forms, contracts, and procedures in order to purchase its property. Therefore, if you're interested in purchasing HUD property, it's advisable to deal directly with a real estate agent who is familiar with selling it.

FORECLOSURES

Another great source of investment is distressed property, such as property in foreclosure. Distressed property has always been a popular investment, especially since it is often sold substantially below market value.

(Incidentally, if you're interested in a more detailed guide to the subject of foreclosures, Contemporary Books publishes my book *Foreclosures: How to Profitably Invest in Distressed Real Estate*.)

The process of foreclosure goes through three phases, and an investor can purchase the distressed property in any one of these phases.

Phase one is when the owner of the property is in default on the loan obligation. During the default phase the lender notifies the owner that it is initiating legal procedures that will eventually lead to a foreclosure sale.

Phase two is the public auction of the property. Unless the loan payments, including late fees and penalties (which are in arrears) are made, the property will be sold at public auction. The lender who is foreclosing initiates the bidding, usually at the price which represents his or her interest, including late fees and penalties. The highest bidder pays off the loan (in cash) and claims the property.

Phase three is the REO stage. If the property does not sell at auction, it reverts to the lender, and if that lender happens to be a financial institution, the property then becomes Real Estate Owned (REO) by the lender.

Purchasing a distressed property during the first phase of foreclosure can often get you a real bargain. However, the many difficulties associated with such a property can often lead you to something you never bargained for. For instance, there may be liens against the property; you may find that, although you were able to buy the property quite easily, you must also buy it back from the IRS, county tax assessor, or some other entity which has attached a lien. Unless you do exhaustive research before getting involved in a foreclosure property, you could get stuck having valuable working capital tied up waiting for liens to be removed or for a title search to be conducted. In the end, your "bargain" may cost a lot more than you had contemplated.

Should a property have problems, you automatically assume them when you purchase it. Property bought during the first phase of foreclosure requires much research and time, and even then you may end up with your funds tied up in escrow for an extended period.

When you purchase property in the second phase, at public auction, you're faced with similar problems, and you must thoroughly investigate the property before you bid. Furthermore, let me again remind you that you are required to pay cash for the property.

It is in the third phase—when the institutional lender has title to the property as REO—that the property emerges as an extremely attractive venture for the investor. But before going any further, be aware of institutional lenders' attitude toward REO: They don't want anything to do with it!

Institutional lenders are in the business of earning money by lending out their funds. They take in savings deposits, then lend these deposits out on long-term real estate loans. Of course, the property itself is used as collateral to secure the loan against the possibility of default by the borrower. Occasionally the lenders are required to foreclose on a property when a loan goes sour. The property is essentially unwanted. The lender would prefer to sell the REO and use the proceeds to fund another loan; therefore, institutional lenders will usually offer attractive terms to an investor to relieve the institution of the unwanted property once it's on the books as REO.

One aspect of REO which makes it a superior investment as compared to property in the other two phases of foreclosure is that all clouds on the title have been removed through the act of foreclosure. In the process of acquiring the property, the financial institution has literally eradicated all outstanding liens, except for back taxes which had to be paid. The lender now owns the property free and clear. If you acquire REO, it will be free of encumbrances, except for deferred maintenance.

You can usually buy REO property with a small down payment. The purchase can often be financed at interest rates below the going market rate, especially since the lender is also the seller and eager to unload the property. Sometimes it's possible to defer the first principal and interest payment up to six months, allowing you to renovate the property and generate some income before the first payment is due; it's not uncommon for the REO buyer to acquire an additional loan to pay for the cost of such renovation. The financial institution will usually assume most of the closing costs.

Remember that everything is very negotiable. Nothing is carved in stone regarding standard procedure for the buying and selling of REO.

To succeed at investing in REO, one needs a special technique for dealing with REO managers. This is not an easy task because there has recently been a great deal of public interest in foreclosure property and potential REO buyers are constantly inquiring.

Typically, an inquiry from an uninformed member of the public is in the form of phone calls to REO departments, asking if any foreclosure property is available. So many people phone in that REO departments now give a stock reply: "Sorry, nothing available."

REO will usually be sold through an established real estate broker and to known investors with whom the lender has previously done business. Thus, if you want to invest in REO, approach the REO department in person and meet its manager. Establishing a personal relationship is the only viable way to have access to these potential bargains.

OTHER SOURCES

In addition to distressed property, classified ads, and the MLS, great bargains can be found just by "cruising" the neighborhood. This means selecting a particular neighborhood where you would like to buy property, driving up and down the streets, and taking notes. This includes noting listed properties as well as FSBOs. While you're at it, keep an eye out for property that looks like it may be for sale. Telltale signs of potential bargains are vacant properties, unattended lawns, boarded-up houses, and homes needing paint.

Once you have a substantial list, you can obtain ownership records from your county courthouse or the property tax collector's office.

In conclusion, also consider inserting an advertisement in the local newspaper, under a category such as "Real Estate Wanted." You'll get a few flaky calls, but you never know: One good bargain could pay for three years of advertising.

PART THREE

Buying Your Second Property, and Beyond

9 HOW TO PYRAMID
YOUR INVESTMENTS

To *pyramid* your investments is to build a massive estate using your initial holdings as the foundation. It's the systematic process of continual investment in additional properties using the earnings and appreciating equities of the initial holdings.

Pyramiding offers the more aggressive realty investor the opportunity to reach the ultimate goal of financial independence. The opportunity to pyramid your investments is brought about by several factors. In every year that you own improved real estate, you'll benefit from the following: increased "sweat equity" brought about by renovations; appreciation caused by inflation; mortgage principal reduction; and tax-free income produced by the investment.

The foundation of your pyramid will probably be the home you already own. But, for those of you just getting started in real estate investing, your objective is to acquire that first investment which will be the foundation of your pyramid.

HOW PYRAMIDING WORKS

Before we get started, some of you might be a little skeptical or bewildered, especially if you haven't already experienced the satisfaction and profitability of owning real property. You may have a tendency to say to yourself, "there's no way that I can pyramid a small amount of savings into a multiple property estate on which I can retire." Believe me: You can do it! Rome wasn't built in a day, and neither will be your retirement

119

estate; you just need to take it one step at a time. You also need to be patient, and let time and appreciation work for you. And finally, you need to persevere and apply the strategies and guidelines emphasized in this book.

To set the stage, certain ground rules must be established. If you recall, in order for you to retire on $18,000 in today's dollars, you would need $54,000 annually, starting 20 years from now. To earn $54,000 annually from realty investments you will need an estate with $432,000 equity in it ($432,000 equity earning 12.5 percent annually yields $54,000). Therefore, in our pyramid plan we will use $432,000 in equity as the objective, based on a 15- to 20-year time span. This may or may not exactly fit in with your plans. In fact, some of you may require more or less income at retirement. Some of you may be able to save more money toward investing, or possibly earn a greater return than what is projected in the pyramid outline. The point is that these projections are based on conservative averages. Even if you cannot save the required minimum, don't be discouraged. You can still do it. You will just have to be more reasonable with your objectives and allow a little more time to reach your ultimate goal.

Now that we've established our objective, let's establish some ground rules:

1. You'll be required to start with initial investment capital of $9000. If you don't have it, you'll either have to allow enough time to save it, or to consider purchasing the initial property using the no-money-down techniques offered in Chapter 3.

2. Beginning now, you'll be required to save at least $3000 in the first year and, because of inflation and salary raises, to save this amount plus six percent more every year for seven years. This is all the savings you'll ever need. After seven years, you'll have enough earnings from previous investments to buy additional properties without using savings.

3. The rate of inflation will average six percent annually.

4. The average rate of appreciation on your holdings will average 6 percent annually.

5. You will earn, on average, 12.5 percent net income annually on your invested dollars.

6. All investments are based on a 10 percent down payment; all exchanges are based on a 20 percent down payment.

7. Closing costs and interest paid on savings are ignored in this outline.

8. All numbers are rounded to the nearest $1000.

THE PYRAMID PLAN IN ACTION

You begin by purchasing a property valued at $90,000 with a $9000 down payment.

By the end of the third year, due to a combination of 6 percent appreciation and mortgage principal reduction, your equity has grown to $28,000. Additionally, you have accumulated $3000 in after-tax cash flows. This $3000, along with $6000 from savings, gives you $9000 to invest in a second property.

Beginning in year six, your equity in the first property has grown to $42,000 and you have accumulated another $2000 in after-tax cash flows. You also have growing equity now worth $21,000 on the second property, and two years of accumulated after-tax cash flows of $2000. This $2000, along with the $2000 from the first property and $5000 from savings, gives you $9000 to invest in a third property.

Beginning in year seven, your equity in the first property is now worth $50,000, which you exchange into a $250,000 property. During year seven, you will earn $6000 in after-tax cash flows on the exchanged property, which we will continue to call property one. (Note that after each exchange, we will continue to refer to the exchanged property by its original number.)

Beginning in year eight, the accumulated earnings from all three properties is $8000. This $8000, along with $1000 from savings, gives you $9000 to invest in a fourth property.

By the end of the ninth year, your equity in the second property is worth $50,000, which you exchange into a $250,000 property.

By the end of the 10th year, you have accumulated after-tax cash flows in excess of $12,000, just from properties one and two. Thus, you invest $9000 in a fifth property, this one valued at $90,000.

By the end of the 11th year, accumulated earnings from properties one and two allow you to invest $9000 in a sixth property (valued at $90,000).

Beginning in year 13, your equity in the third property is now worth $50,000, which you exchange into a $250,000 property.

Beginning in year 14, your equity in the fourth property is now worth $50,000, which you exchange into a $250,000 property.

Beginning in year 15, your equity in property one, due to a combination of 6 percent appreciation and mortgage principal reduction, has grown to $220,000, which you exchange into a $1,100,000 property.

After 15 years, you will make one last exchange. Your equity in property two is now worth $170,000, which you exchange into an $850,000 property.

In 15 years, you have parlayed an initial $9000 investment into a retirement estate far exceeding the objective of $432,000 in equities. This is how fortunes are made in real estate. What you have witnessed is actually a very conservative model, using a moderate 6 percent appreciation factor—while most areas of the country experience 8 percent or more. Now, for an illustrated example of the pyramid plan we discussed—$702,000 in equities in fifteen years—see Figure 9.1.

The results in Figure 9.1 are very realistic. It's up to you to achieve them. You only have to perservere, and use your initial holdings as a stepping stone to reach the ultimate goal: a huge retirement estate that offers you total financial freedom.

HOW TO TRADE YOUR PROPERTY

There are several methods of working out the mechanics of a trade. The most common method is to trade on the basis of free-and-clear valuations, then figure out the terms of financ-

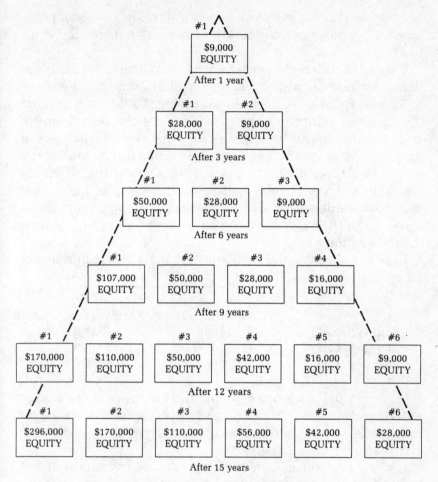

Figure 9.1 Illustrated Pyramid Plan

ing and boot. The term "boot" means something given in lieu of cash in an exchange to equalize value.

As an example of this method, let's say you own property "B" valued at $80,000 with a loan of $50,000. You want to trade it for property "A" valued at $150,000 with a loan of $100,000. The difference between equities of the two properties is $20,000 in favor of property "A." Thus property "B," with a sales price of $80,000, would be traded plus a boot of $20,000 for property "A." The boot in this example could be something of value such as a boat or car; or the owner of property "A" could carry a second mortgage to balance the equities.

The price differential between the exchanged properties is not important; only the difference in equities is important.

To qualify for a tax-deferred exchange, the IRS requires that the assumed mortgages be larger than the ones being given, and that the equity be larger than that being given. Also, it must be a "like for like" exchange. This means you must trade for another real estate investment which you will hold for investment purposes. You could not, for example, trade your principal residence for a 10-unit rental building or vice-versa. Finally, the IRS requires that you receive no cash or boot in the transaction.

Let's see if properties "A" and "B" meet the requirements for a tax-deferred exchange.

	Property "A"	Property "B"
Selling price	$150,000	$80,000
Mortgage balances	100,000	50,000
Cash required	50,000	30,000

A trade-up, which our example illustrates, qualifies for tax deferment because the mortgages being assumed are larger than those given, the equity is also larger than that being given, and no boot was given.

It's also possible to have multiple exchanges, instead of just two. Of course, the more properties involved, the more complicated the exchange. If you have a complicated exchange, it's advisable to hire a CPA and an attorney. Their combined efforts will probably protect your interests and save you money.

You can defer tax indefinitely on your gains, as long as you continue to enter into a tax-deferred exchange every time you trade properties. You may never have to pay tax on the gains in your property. Upon death, your heirs inherit the property at market value, not at your adjusted cost basis.

It's certainly true that minimizing taxes, or deferring them altogether, can greatly enhance profits and increase the investor's pyramiding potential.

10 HOW TO SAVE ON INCOME TAXES

Entire books have been written on the subject of income taxes. It is the objective of this chapter to unravel and simplify the complicated tax laws that pertain only to real estate. This should assist you in tax planning and help you save money on income taxes.

Real property ownership offers the average family tax shelter benefits that do not exist with other common forms of investment. Recent tax reform has eliminated or reduced tax shelter benefits on most other investments. Although real estate's ability to shelter income also has been reduced, it still remains the preferred tax shelter.

HOMEOWNER TAX SAVINGS

You can avoid or defer tax on the gain from the sale of your home, depending on certain conditions and your age.

Deferring Tax on the Sale of a Residence

You can defer tax on the gain from the sale of your home if you meet the following three tests:

1. Principal residence test. This test requires that you have used your old house as your principal residence and you now use, or intend to use, your new house as a principal residence. For tax-deferral purposes, only one principal residence is allowed at any one time. You cannot defer tax on the profitable sale of a principal residence by buying a summer cottage, nor can you defer the tax on the sale of a second home.

2. *Time test.* This test requires that within two years of the sale of your old house you buy (or build) and use your new house as your principal residence.

3. *Investment test.* This test requires that you buy or build a house for an amount equal to, or more than, the amount you received from the sale of the old house. If the replacement house costs less, part or all of the gain is taxed. Tax deferring is mandatory when you qualify under the above three tests.

Exchanging houses or trading is considered the same as a sale for tax deferral purposes. If you make an even exchange, or pay additional cash, there is no tax on the trade. However, if you receive cash in the trade for the replacement house, you generally realize a taxable gain.

Tax-Free Residence Sale if You're Age 55 or Older

You can avoid tax on profits up to $125,000 once in your lifetime, if you are age 55 or older when you sell or exchange your principal residence. In order to claim this exclusion, you must:

1. elect to avoid tax;
2. be age 55 or older before the date of sale; and
3. for at least three years prior to the sale have owned and occupied the house as your principal residence.

You cannot use this exclusion when you sell only a partial interest in your home.

If you and your spouse own the home jointly and file a joint return in the year of the sale, only one of you need meet the age requirement of 55 or older, and need qualify under ownership and residency requirements.

Use caution when taking the tax-free election. Because this is a once-in-a-lifetime exclusion, consider instead using the tax-deferral method, when the gain from the sale of your home is substantially less than the $125,000 exclusion and you plan to reinvest the proceeds in a replacement home. If, for example, you did qualify for the $125,000 exclusion, and after the sale of your home the gain was only $15,000 and you elected to exclude it, you will have used up your once-in-a-lifetime exclusion. You could defer this gain if you buy a replacement house at a cost equal to or more than the sales price of the old house. Then, when you later sell the replacement house without a further home purchase, you can make the election to exclude the gain.

Interest Deductions and Refinancing

Highlights

1. Mortgage interest is deductible on two homes only, capped at $1 million.
2. Interest deductions on investments are limited to the amount of net investment income.
3. Interest deduction for a home equity loan is limited to $100,000.

Generally, the points you pay to refinance your principal residence are not deductible, regardless of how you pay them, if they're not paid in connection with the purchase or improvement of the home. However, a portion of points is deductible if you use a part of the proceeds to make an improvement on your principal residence and you pay the costs out of your private funds (rather than out of the proceeds of the new loan). You may either deduct in full the amount apportioned for the improvement in the year you pay it, or you may deduct the apportioned amount over the life of the loan.

Deductions for interest paid on refinancing your mortgage are allowed up to the purchase price of your property, plus the cost of any improvements you've made. You may not claim a deduction for interest paid on that portion of a mortgage loan that, at the time the debt was incurred, is greater than the costs of improvements and purchase price of the property. The tax law does make an exception to this rule: You can deduct interest on that part of a mortgage or equity loan that exceeds the purchase price and cost improvements, if you use the excess loan proceeds to pay educational or medical expenses. On the other hand, if you were to take out a personal loan (not secured by a residence) to send your son or daughter to college, then the interest on that loan is not deductible as home mortgage interest.

The rule for limiting deduction on the home's appreciation was implemented to prevent taxpayers from borrowing against home appreciation, using the money to pay off their consumer purchases, and then deducting the interest.

Let's assume you decide to refinance your home, which is worth $100,000. You originally paid $40,000 and have made $10,000 in improvements. The lender will allow you to refinance up to $80,000, but you may write off the interest on only $50,000 ($40,000 purchase price plus $10,000 in home improvements).

If you accept the lender's maximum loan of $80,000, the interest charged by the lender on the $30,000 (the amount in excess of purchase price plus improvements) is nondeductible personal interest if used for any purposes other than trade or business or investment. However, if the excess $30,000 is used to pay educational or medical expenses, all the interest on the $80,000 loan is tax-deductible.

What home improvements qualify to increase the amount you can borrow? A home improvement is generally considered to include all expenditures that add value to your home and last for an extended period, such as a swimming pool, new roof, new patio or deck, siding, built-in appliances, built-in cabinets, alarm system, hot water heater, new sidewalk, replacement windows, insulation, and certain landscaping.

What mortgage loans are affected by these rules? All home loans that originated after August 16, 1986 are subject to the latest tax laws. Home mortgage loans that were outstanding on this date will not be affected unless they exceed the fair market value of the home at that date. Also, the mortgage interest on one additional home, such as a vacation home, will qualify for the mortgage interest deduction. To qualify for a vacation home, see rules for vacation homes (the next topic in this chapter).

RULES FOR VACATION HOMES

For tax purposes, you should remember: (1) Mortgage interest is deductible only on your first and second homes, capped at $1 million (1988 and after). (2) Deductible losses on rented vacation homes are limited to $25,000 (this cap is reduced when adjusted gross income is over $100,000).

The tax law prohibits most homeowners from deducting losses (expenses in excess of income) while renting out a personal vacation home. A vacation home can be a condominium, apartment, house trailer, motor home, boat, or house. The following tests, based on days of rental and personal usage, will determine whether you are allowed losses:

1. If the vacation home is rented for fewer than 15 days, you cannot deduct expenses allocated to the rental (except for interest and real estate taxes). If you sell and realize a profit on the rental, the profit is not taxable if the conditions for tax deferral or tax-free sale are met.

2. If the vacation home is rented for 15 days or more, you have to determine if your personal use of the home exceeds a 14-day or 10-percent time test (10 percent of the number of days the home is rented). If it does, then you are considered to have used the home as a residence during the year, and rental expenses are deductible only to the extent of gross rental income. Therefore, if gross rental income exceeds expenses, the operating gain is fully taxable.

3. If you rent the vacation home for 15 days or more, but your rental usage is less than the 14-day/10 percent test, you are not considered to have made personal use of the residence during the year. In this case, expenses in excess of gross rental income may be deductible. Previous federal tax court cases have allowed loss deductions when the owner made little personal use of the vacation home and proved to have bought the house to earn a profitable amount in resale.

RULES FOR DEPRECIATION

The main points are:

1. Residential rentals are depreciated over 27.5 years; commercial rentals over 31.5 years.
2. Only the straight-line method of depreciation is allowed on income property.
3. Vehicles are depreciated over five years.
4. Most machinery and equipment is depreciated over seven years.
5. Personal property is depreciated using the double-declining-balance method.

Depreciation is the percentage of reduction in value of an asset over its physical life. It is strictly a bookkeeping entry, not an out-of-pocket expense to the investor.

Generally speaking, if you buy property to use in a trade or business or to earn rent or royalty income and the property has a useful life of more than one year, you cannot deduct its entire cost in one year. You must spread the cost over several years and deduct a part of it each year. For most types of property, this is called depreciation.

What Can Be Depreciated?

Many different kinds of property can be depreciated, such as machinery, buildings, vehicles, patents, copyrights, furniture, and equipment. Property is depreciated if it meets all three of these tests:

1. It must be used in business or held for the production of income (for example, to earn rent or royalty income).
2. It must have a useful life that can be determined, and its useful life must be longer than one year. The useful life of a piece of real property is an estimate of how long you can expect to use it in your business or to earn rent or royalty income from it.

3. It must be something that wears out, decays, gets used up, becomes obsolete, or loses value from natural causes.

Depreciable property may be tangible (that is, it can be seen or touched) or intangible. Intangible property includes such items as a copyright or franchise. Depreciable property may be personal or real. Personal property is property that is not real estate, such as machinery or equipment. Real property is land and generally anything that is erected on, growing on, or attached to the land. However, land itself is not depreciable.

Depreciation not only serves a purpose in determining taxable income, but is also the essence of why real estate has been a tax shelter. Historically, real estate investors have been able to earn substantial net income, free of taxes from their properties, while actually showing taxable losses that could be written off against salary income. This is the tax-shelter benefit of real estate, because the taxable loss (actually a net gain, or profit) can shelter salary income from other sources.

Figuring Depreciation

It is important to understand the two basic types of assets, each of which is depreciable under different rules. You can obtain valuable tax savings by carefully drawing distinctions between these two types of property because, although real property is limited to straight-line depreciation, personal property can be depreciated using accelerated methods of depreciation.

Depreciating Buildings

Residential real property is depreciated using the straight-line method over a useful life of 27.5 years (31.5 years for nonresidential property such as office buildings and shopping centers). In the month you purchase, or put the building in use, you are required to use one-half month's depreciation deduction. This is called the midmonth convention.

Residential property is defined as a building with 80 percent or more of its rental income derived from dwelling units. A dwelling unit is defined as an apartment or house used to provide living accommodations. This does not include hotels or motels which rent more than half of their capacity on a temporary basis. If you reside in one of the apartments, a fair rental value can be allocated to your living unit.

Depreciating Land Improvements

Certain land improvements are depreciated over 15 years using the 150 percent declining-balance method. Conversion to the straight-line method, at a time when deductions can be maximized, is also allowed. Depreciable land improvements are items such as bridges, roads, sidewalks, and landscaping. Sewer pipes are depreciated over a 20-year period. Buildings and their improvements are not allowed under this method.

Depreciating Equipment and Fixtures

Personal property, such as vehicles, equipment, or furniture, is generally written off by using the double-declining-balance method over a five- or seven-year period. For example, most cars and light trucks are depreciated over five years. Most office furniture, fixtures, and equipment (desks, safes, and certain communication equipment) are depreciated over seven years. In addition, only one-half year of depreciation deduction is allowed in the year the asset was purchased or built (the half-year convention). The half-year convention also applies to real property. (Note that the accelerated methods of 150 percent and double-declining balance are calculated at one-and-a-half and twice, respectively, the rate of the straight-line method.) Table 10.1 illustrates how the declining-balance method works for five-year property.

The tax law permits a switch to the straight-line method when the switch will provide a larger deduction. In the fifth year, the double-declining-balance method would provide a deduction of $830 (40 percent × $2074). Switching to the straight-line method in the fifth year provides a deduction of $1382 ($2074 of costs not yet written off, divided by the 1.5 years remaining in the depreciation period). The half-year convention causes the depreciation period to be extended to a sixth year.

Table 10.1 Example of Double Declining-Balance Method

Year	(Declining Balance) Cost	Rate of Depreciation %	Amount of Depreciation
1	$12,000	40 × .5	$2,400
2	9,600	40	3,840
3	5,760	40	2,304
4	3,456	40	1,382
5	2,074	—	1,382
6	692	—	692
			$12,000

The calculations for seven-year property and the 150 percent declining-balance method of depreciation are similar, except that under the 150 percent method, one-and-a-half times the straight-line method is used (30 percent instead of 40 percent) in the "rate of depreciation" column.

RULES FOR PASSIVE INCOME AND LOSSES

The highlights to consider are:

1. Deductible losses on real estate are limited to $25,000, reduced for adjusted gross income over $100,000.
2. Losses are not deductible under the $25,000 cap unless you actively participate in managing the property.
3. Losses in excess of $25,000 can be used only to offset gains from other passive investments.

A passive activity is any activity that involves the conduct of any trade or business in which you do not materially participate. Any rental activity is a passive activity even if you materially participate in it. A trade or business includes any activity involving research or experimentation and, to the extent provided in the IRS regulations, any activity in connection with a trade or business or any activity for which a deduction is allowed as an expense for the production of income. You are considered to participate materially if you are involved in the operation of the activity on a regular, continuous, and substantial basis. Participation by your spouse will be considered in determining whether you materially participate.

For tax years beginning after 1986, your deductions from passive activities may only be used to offset your income from passive activities. Any excess deductions result in a "passive-activity loss" and may not be deducted against your other income but may be carried over and applied against passive income in future years. In addition, any allowable credits from passive activity may only be used to offset future tax liability allocable to your passive activities.

Here's an illustration of the impact of the new passive-loss limitations brought about by the Tax Reform Act of 1986. Assume that an investor with an aversion to paying income taxes has purchased real estate tax shelters in the past from a syndicator for the purpose of sheltering other income. Other sources of income are salary as an executive of a corporation, dividends and interest, and investments in several syndicated tax shelters.

Salary	$150,000
Dividends	21,000
Interest	14,000
Tax-shelter losses	($183,000)
Taxable income before exemptions	$ 2,000

After taking into consideration the personal exemption, the investor in this example would in fact owe no tax. The income under passive-income rules falls into three categories: Salary of $150,000 under the active income category, dividends and interest under the portfolio category, and tax shelter losses under the passive-income category. Figure 10.1 gives examples of the three categories.

Under the latest tax reform, this investor will generally not be allowed to use the losses from the passive-income category to offset income and gains from the other categories. Therefore, under the tax reform provisions, the investor will no

Active	Passive	Portfolio
Employee wages	Most rental real estate	Interest
Primary trade or business	Net leased realty	Dividends
Real estate development	Limited partnership	REIT (Real Estate Investment Trust) distributions
Active retailer	No material participation	Royalties
Consultant		

Figure 10.1 Example of Three Types of Income for Passive-Loss Rules

longer be able to avoid paying taxes. Total income will be $185,000 ($150,000 active income and $35,000 portfolio income), and in 1988 he or she must pay a tax of $51,800 ($185,000 × 28 percent), overlooking common itemized deductions. This dramatic result is exactly what Congress sought to achieve when it made changes in investment taxation under the Tax Reform Act of 1986.

Certain Passive-Income Losses Can Offset Other Income

As mentioned before, an interest in real estate rental activity, regardless of degree of participation, will not be considered an active business. This means that losses from real estate investments are only allowed to offset income and gains from other passive investments. Therefore, real estate losses cannot shelter wage or active business income. However, there is a major exception to this rule, one that assists moderate-income taxpayers who invest in real estate.

Certain investors can apply passive-income losses to wage earnings or income from an active business. In order to qualify for this real estate loss exception (up to a maximum of $25,000), the investor must meet both an income and a participation test. The investor's adjusted gross income (AGI) must be less than $150,000. The entire $25,000 loss allowance is permitted for taxpayers with AGIs up to $100,000. Over this amount, the allowance is reduced by 50 percent of the amount by which the AGI exceeds $100,000. Thus, if the AGI is $150,000, the allowance is zero.

The other requirement for this loss allowance is that the investor must "actively participate." (This rule is not so stringent as other participation tests, as you will soon see.) To get the benefit of up to $25,000 in tax losses, the investor is required to meet the following two tests: (1) The investor must own at least 10 percent of the value of the activity during the entire year that the allowance is claimed; (2) The investor is required to make management decisions or arrange for others to provide such services. It is not necessary for the investor to do certain things directly, such as repairs or approval of prospective tenants. The hiring of a repair person and a rental agent does not violate the participation test; however, take caution if you hire a management company to operate the property. The property management agreement should clearly state that you, the investor, are involved in the decision-making process.

Passive-Income Losses Are Carried Forward

Those losses the investor couldn't use during one tax year are carried forward as "suspended losses" and used in one of two ways: (1) If the investor has unused losses incurred in prior years and carried forward, those losses apply against income or gains in the passive-income category in future years. Under previous tax law the losses would have been used to shelter income from other sources. However, under current law they can only be used to shelter income in later years for the same or other passive-income investments. (2) Unused suspended losses from prior years can be used to reduce any gain you realize when you dispose of your investment.

In determining income or loss from an activity, do not consider (A) any gross income from interest, dividends, annuities, or royalties not derived in the ordinary course of trade or business; (B) expenses (other than interest) that are clearly and directly allocable to such other income; (C) interest expenses properly allocable to such income; and (D) gain or loss from the disposition of property producing such income or held for investment. Any interest in a passive activity is not treated as property held for investment. In addition, you do not include wages, salaries, professional fees, or other amounts received as compensation for services rendered as income from a passive activity.

Effective Dates of the Passive-Loss Rules

Finally, you have to take into consideration the dates when these new rules went into effect. Beginning in 1987, they are effective for all losses. However, for investments made prior to October 22, 1986, when the Tax Reform Act was enacted, these new rules are phased in over a five-year period. Therefore, for investments made before this date, you are allowed losses to offset earned or portfolio income according to the following percentages:

- 1987   65 percent
- 1988   40 percent
- 1989   20 percent
- 1990   10 percent
- 1991 and after   0 percent

CAPITAL GAINS

Capital gains are now taxed as ordinary income. Before tax reform, you could exclude from taxes 60 percent of the gain if the asset was held six months or longer. Now, for tax years 1988 and after, all capital gains are taxed at a maximum rate of 28 percent. See Table 10.2 for income tax brackets for 1988 and later.

HOW TO FIGURE THE ADJUSTED COST BASIS

After taking depreciation allowances all these years, you now have to give them back to the IRS. When you sell income property, the adjusted cost basis (ACB) has to be adjusted by the amount of depreciation you've already taken. How much after-tax profit you earned after the sale is dependent on three factors. The original purchase price is adjusted by these three factors to attain profit subject to tax. They are: (1) the amount of depreciation already taken; (2) any capital improvements made to the property; and (3) the costs incurred while acquiring and selling the property.

Table 10.2 Income Tax Brackets 1988 and Later

Tax Rate (%)	Married, Filing Joint Return	Married, Filing Separate Return	Heads of Household	Single Individuals
15	0–$29,750	0–$14,875	0–$23,900	0–$17,850
28	over $29,750	over $14,875	over $23,900	over $17,850

Let's say you owned an income property five years, and during that time you were able to take a depreciation allowance each year. Now, since you sold the property, the IRS makes you give back the depreciation you took during the five years of ownership. They get it by reducing your cost basis in the property by the amount of depreciation allowance already taken.

However, on the brighter side, the IRS does allow you to increase your cost basis by adding to it any capital improvements you made while owning the property. You can also add the transaction costs you incurred in order to buy and sell the property, such as a sales commission.

Figure 10.2 shows how to calculate the ACB.

INSTALLMENT SALES

When you sell real estate and carry back a loan, it's considered an installment sale. If you realize the entire sales price in the year of the sale, then it's not an installment sale.

How much of the deferred payments under an installment sale are taxable? The rules state that to determine the taxable amount of income on each payment, the gross profit ratio is applied to each payment received. The gross profit ratio is figured by dividing the taxable gain (gross profit) by the total sales price.

As an example, suppose you sell your residence for $200,000 (you paid $50,000 for it 10 years ago). To consummate the sale, you carried back a second mortgage. You have a taxable gain of $150,000. To find out the gross profit ratio, divide the $150,000 taxable gain by the total sales price of $200,000, resulting in a 75 percent gross profit ratio. Therefore, 75 percent of the down payment, and of each deferred payment, must be reported as income.

In the event the buyer in the above example were to assume an existing mortgage, the total sales price—for the purpose of this calculation—would be reduced by the amount of that mortgage. For example, if the buyer assumes an existing mortgage of $25,000 in addition to making deferred payments to you on a second mortgage, the total sales price would be reduced by $25,000 and different calculations have to be made to find the gross profit ratio.

Total Sales Price	$200,000
Mortgage Assumed	− 25,000
Adjusted Sales Price	$175,000

Under these circumstances, the gross profit ratio is 85.71 percent ($150,000 taxable gain divided by the adjusted sales price of $175,000).

ADMINISTRATIVE CHANGES CAUSED BY TAX REFORM

You should be aware of certain new requirements for investing in tax shelters and reporting rental income.

Let's say you purchased a building five years ago for $100,000 and sold it for $150,000. To figure your ACB, you deduct depreciation already taken from the purchase price. Then you add in all transaction costs and capital improvements made. See the following:

Purchase Price	$100,000	
Less: Depreciation allowance	20,000	
taken	80,000	
Plus: Capital improvements	−0−	
Transaction Costs	8,000	
Adjusted Cost Basis (ACB)	88,000	
Selling Price		$150,000
Less: ACB		− 88,000
Profit Subject to Tax		$ 62,000

Figure 10.2 Adjusted Cost Basis

Registration of Tax Shelters

A tax shelter must be registered with the IRS, and the registration must take place no later than the day on which interests in it are first offered for sale to the investors. The principal organizer of the shelter is responsible for the filing. However, if this person fails to do so, another member of the shelter can be responsible.

Under registration requirements the seller must provide each investor with the tax shelter identification number issued by the IRS, and this number is reported on the tax return. The IRS can assess penalties for failing to meet these requirements.

Reporting Rental Income and Deductions

Rental income and expenses are reported on Schedule E of your income tax return. You report the gross amount received, then deduct such expenses as mortgage interest, property taxes, maintenance costs, and depreciation. The net profit is added to your other taxable income. If you realize a loss, you can reduce the amount of your other taxable income within certain limitations. (See passive-loss limitation rules in this chapter.)

If you use the cash basis as your accounting method, you report rental income for the year in which you receive payment.

Security deposits are treated as trust funds and are not reported as income. However, if your tenant breaches the lease agreement, then you are entitled to use the security deposit as rent; if so, you report it as income.

CHECKLIST OF DEDUCTIONS FROM RENTAL INCOME

Real Estate Taxes

Property taxes are deductible, but special assessments for paving roads, sewers, or other improvements are not. They are added to the cost of the land.

Depreciation

Be sure to deduct the appropriate depreciation allowance on income property; this is the tax shelter benefit of real estate ownership.

Maintenance Expenses

Repairs, pool service, heating, lighting, water, gas, electricity, telephone, and other service costs are all tax-deductible expenses.

Management Expenses

Include, for example, the cost of stationery and postage stamps, or the total cost of a management service.

Traveling Expenses

These include travel to and from properties for repairs, rent collection, or showing vacancies.

Legal Expenses

These include the costs incurred while evicting a tenant. Expenses incurred in negotiating long-term leases are considered capital expenditures and are deductible over the term of the lease.

Interest Expenses

This includes interest on mortgages and other indebtedness related to the property.

Advertising Expenses

This includes the cost of vacancy signs and newspaper advertising.

Insurance Expenses

This includes the cost of premiums for fire and casualty loss.

Note the difference between repair expenses and improvements. Only incidental repair and maintenance costs are deductible against rental income. Improvement and replacement costs are treated differently. Improvements or repairs that add value or prolong the life of the property are considered capital improvements and may not be deducted, but they may be added to the cost basis of the property and may then be depreciated. For example, the cost to repair the roof of a rental property is considered an expense and is deducted against rental income. However, the cost to *replace* the roof is considered an improvement (it adds value and prolongs the physical life of the property) and is therefore added to the cost of the property and then depreciated.

SUMMARY

Congress designed the 1986 Tax Reform Act with the intention of implementing a doctrine of fairness, and at the same time it attempted to simplify the overall tax system. It did achieve a certain amount of fairness when it reduced individual tax rates. Nevertheless, it did not by any means simplify the tax system. In fact, it made it more complex.

Under the new regulations, special care must be taken by borrowers. Deductions for interest paid on loans other than mortgages depend upon how the borrowed money is used. Under the old law, interest was generally deductible no matter how the proceeds from a loan were spent.

Under the new rules, taxpayers who borrow must trace how they use the loan proceeds from the day they take out the loan until the day they repay it. In 1988, proceeds must be used for home improvement, education costs, and medical bills. After 1988, there are no restrictions.

Under the new rules, more forms and stricter accounting practices are required of the taxpayer. In order to comply under the new complex system, the following procedures are suggested to simplify record-keeping and to avoid losing deductions because of improper record-keeping methods.

• Maintain separate accounts for personal, business, and investment use.

- Be sure that debts incurred for investments can be traced to those investments. (Note the 15-day rule, which states that the taxpayer who spends the proceeds of a loan within 15 days qualifies for the deduction; however, if the loan proceeds sit longer than 15 days, the IRS will base the deduction eligibility on the first purchase made from the borrowed funds.)
- As opposed to other forms of loans, consider home-equity loans, which are fully tax-deductible and don't require as much record-keeping.
- Refrain from writing checks on stock margin accounts, except for buying stock.

11 PROPERTY MANAGEMENT —WITHOUT HASSLES

Welcome to the concept of property management—without hassles. That's what this chapter is all about—how to get the most out of your realty holdings with the least amount of difficulty.

I like to call it the "lazy person's guide to property management." That's because it's a do-it-yourself guide to simple and efficient real estate management. I'll show you how to avoid the common nuisances—the ones that the uninformed and inexperienced rental owners face every day and don't know how to handle correctly.

Poorly managed real estate can drain your resources and be a burdensome daily chore. Bad management is not only a drain on your finances, it's also a waste of your time and energy. It can turn a potentially good investment into a nightmare. On the other hand, when you do things the right way, not only will you make the most from them, you can just about put your realty holdings on automatic pilot and take an extended, well-deserved vacation.

REASONS WHY PEOPLE SHY AWAY FROM REAL ESTATE

If owning income property is so profitable, why aren't more people landlords? The answer lies primarily in the fact that ignorance breeds inefficiency. Uneducated landlords not only rent to the wrong people, they also mismanage their funds and defer proper maintenance on their properties. Non-paying or habitually late-paying tenants are a never-ending headache. Mismanagement of funds can eventually cause loss of the property through foreclosure. And if a property is poorly maintained, it not only doesn't receive the amount of income it would if properly maintained, it also loses market value.

There are other reasons, such as divorce, death in the family, or loss of employment; but primarily it's ignorance, or a lack of skill to do the job the right way, that causes people to shy away from managing real estate.

BEING A SUCCESSFUL LANDLORD IS NO ACCIDENT

Good management requires you to know how to do things correctly. The skills of rent collection, qualifying tenants, showing vacancies, and maintaining a budget don't require hard work, but they require you to take the time to learn proficiency at these skills.

Good management is also about managing people. This includes overseeing a resident manager if you have a multi-unit building, or properly handling tenants of single-family rentals. Whatever the case, you must manage people, and they in turn manage your property for you. Then, most of your management work can be done over the phone—the lazy person's way.

MANAGING MULTI-UNIT BUILDINGS

Whether you own a small duplex or a large 20-unit building, someone has to be responsible "on site." The key here is to make someone responsible: someone living on the property to show vacancies, collect rents, and generally oversee the property.

In a 20-unit building, the person responsible is the resident manager. But even in a two-unit building, you should still have a manager responsible for certain duties, such as showing vacancies and maintaining the exterior grounds. In this way the owner is relieved of certain menial duties by delegating them to the resident manager. (See additional material about the resident manager later in this chapter.)

Furnished Versus Unfurnished Units

Generally, if you are renting single-family houses, it is to your advantage to keep your units unfurnished. If you supply furniture, you can of course charge more in rent for the use of that furniture; however, it then becomes your responsibility to maintain and insure if against theft and fire damage. The major disadvantage of supplying furniture to your tenants is the fact that it creates more turnover. It is very easy to get up and move away from a rented home that is completely furnished. On the other hand, a rented home where the tenant supplies his or her own furnishings requires much more effort to occupy and vacate. Invariably, once a tenant takes the time, effort, and expense to move all his or her belongings into a home, it is very likely he or she plans to stay awhile.

However, certain types of rental units require furniture in order to maintain a high occupancy rate. If you own single or studio-type apartments (these tend to thrive on a more transient clientele), supplying adequate furnishings would be to your advantage.

Appliances

Items such as refrigerators, washers, dryers, and dishwashers are expensive to buy and maintain, but when they are offered as an amenity with your rental unit, they offer saleability to your rental. If you have the opportunity to buy these appliances at bargain prices (as part of the purchase of the entire investment property) by all means do so. The responsibility to maintain and repair such appliances can mostly be turned over to your tenants via the "no hassle $100-deductible repair clause" inserted into your rental agreement. This clause states that "the first $100 in repair of the rented property, including appliances, is the tenant's responsibility." (More on the "no hassle" clause later in this section.)

If you own a multi-unit apartment building with nine or more rental units, you have to consider whether to supply a laundry facility with coin-operated washers and dryers, and if so, whether you should buy or lease the equipment. In smaller buildings (eight rental units or less), supplying washers and dryers is not economically feasible because usage would not pay for the cost of the utilities to run the machines.

Should you buy the coin-operated equipment, they would probably pay for themselves within two years. That's the good part. However, you have to maintain the equipment and be responsible for vandalism and unauthorized removal of coins.

On the other hand, you could lease your laundry equipment from a reputable rental company. In this way the leasing company would be responsible for supplying and maintaining the equipment, while at the same time collecting coins from the machines. Generally, when you lease laundry equipment, the leasing company retains 60 percent of the gross receipts and remits the remaining 40 percent to the lessee. Precautionary measures can be taken so that a responsible person oversees the removal of coins from the leased equipment, in order to help eliminate the temptation of skimming from the coin boxes.

Utilities and Trash Removal

For the tenant who rents a single-family residence or condominium, it is his or her responsibility to pay for utilities and trash removal. However, in most apartment buildings—especially the later models—there are separate meters for gas and electricity consumption, and the respective companies bill the individual tenants; the owner of the building is responsible for paying the water bill (for the common area only, not the individual units). When separate meters are not available for water, gas, and electricity, the owner must add the cost of these items to the rent. Furthermore, trash removal from multi-unit buildings is best paid for by the owner, so as to maintain a cleaner common area around the building and avoid friction with the tenants over whose responsibility it is.

SHOWING AND RENTING VACANT UNITS

This section shows you a step-by-step procedure for taking a vacant unit and filling it with a good, qualified, paying tenant. While your particular vacant unit might be the greatest rental in the city, a vacant house or apartment will remain unoccupied indefinitely if the public doesn't know it is available. On the other hand, if you rent the unit to an undesirable, non-paying deadbeat, you'll soon wish it were vacant! The surest way to financial suicide, or at least a migraine headache, is to continually rent to flaky people who won't pay. There are enough qualified prospects to fill your vacancy; all you have to do is advertise for them and then properly qualify them.

Advertising

Prospecting for tenants is best accomplished through posted vacancy signs and by placing classified advertising in your local newspaper. Vacancy signs must be precise and to the point, qualifying the prospective tenant to a certain degree. For example, "Vacancy, 1-Bedroom, Adults Only," or "Vacancy, 2-Bedroom, Kids OK." By stating certain facts about the available unit, you will eliminate a lot of unqualified prospects who are looking for something you don't have. Your signs should be legible and large enough so they can easily be seen from a passing vehicle. Place your vacancy signs on either side of your building, or post them on the lawn near the busiest street for maximum exposure.

Classified advertising should also be precise and qualifying in order to eliminate unnecessary calls from unqualified people. The four basic principles of good advertising are "AIDA"—the four letters stand for ATTENTION (Your headline should attract specific prospects), INTEREST (You should expand the headline and offer a benefit to the prospect that makes him read the rest of the ad), DESIRE (With good descriptive copy, make the prospect want what you have to offer), and ACTION (Ask for the action by making it easy for the prospect to respond to your offer).

ATTENTION . . . It could be a heading like "Newly Decorated," or "Large 3-Bedroom." The purpose of the attention heading is to get the reader to distinguish your ad from the numerous other ads in the same column. Another example would be "Free Rent for One Month." (This type of ad might be used in a rental market already oversupplied with available units. Free rent would definitely get more attention than the other ads in the same column.)

INTEREST . . . To develop interest one should offer a benefit like "2 fireplaces," or "Newly Carpeted," or "Great Ocean View" to entice the reader to read the rest of your advertisement.

DESIRE . . . This should describe precisely what you have to offer, such as "2 Bedroom, Kids OK, $375," or "1 Bedroom, Adults Only, Pool, $350."

ACTION . . . This can simply be a phone number for the prospect to call and inquire.

Classified advertising is printed under specific headings, so there is no need to duplicate information that is already available. In other words, it is not necessary to state that your apartment is unfurnished when your ad is running under the column "Unfurnished Apartments," or to state that your house is downtown when your ad is running under a column denoting that area of your city.

Begin your ad with the location, then the type of unit. For example:

NEAR DOWNTOWN . . . 2 bedroom, 1 bath, patio and large fenced yard, kids and pets ok. $475. Call 555–1212.

By beginning your ad with the location, you qualify people right from the start. People look for rentals usually based on areas in which they want to live. Anyone looking for a two-bedroom apartment in the downtown area will respond to this ad; anyone looking for a three-bedroom in a different area will look elsewhere.

After a full description, including any particular features, close the ad with the amount of rent you're charging and a phone number to call. The amount of rent is important because you again qualify the prospect. If you're charging more rent than the prospect can afford to pay, he or she won't bother to call.

The following was a sample advertisement that proved very effective. It ran in my local newspaper under the section "Unfurnished Condominiums For Rent":

> RENT WITH BUY OPTION . . . Spring Mt. & Jones, 3 Bedroom, 2 Bath, neat & clean, beautifully landscaped and decorated, with tennis cts, pool & jacuzzi. $695. Call 555–1212.

Showing the Vacant Unit

At this point, your advertisement is running in the local paper and your vacancy signs are strategically located on the available unit. It is imperative that the vacant unit be ready to be shown, which means it should be neat and clean throughout. If you are renting an occupied unit that will be vacated shortly, inform the occupants of your intentions. Request that they keep the unit tidy so that you can show the unit to prospects.

While you're showing the unit, point out features of the unit such as storage, cabinets, view, and so on. Do not bring up what you might consider to be negative, because what may be a negative aspect to some may not be to others. Make sure you know the exact square footage of the available unit.

The prospects, if they are interested in the unit, will usually begin by asking questions concerning schools (What are they? What are their reputations?), transportation (Do you know the bus schedules?), shopping, and so on—questions which you should be prepared to answer. If you do not know the schools in the area, for example, find out about them.

Renting the Unit

At this point your prospective tenants have seen the unit and have decided to rent it. What do you do now? First, get as big a deposit as you can, and do not accept a check for it. Your prospects could stop payment on the check once they leave the premises, and you could be stuck with a worthless check. Accept only cash or a money order for the deposit, and make sure it's for at least $100. Anything less could entice your prospects into not upholding their obligation, should they find something they preferred before moving into your rental.

After receiving the deposit and giving your prospects a receipt, have them complete an Application to Rent (See Appendix [Forms]). Be sure your prospects fill out the application completely, because you will use this information later to determine whether you will accept them as tenants. Once they have completed the application, check for omissions; if there are none, tell your tenants that you will phone them once you make a decision on their application.

Qualifying the Prospective Tenant

From the Application to Rent, you now have to determine whether it would be wise to accept the applicants as tenants. Essentially what you are looking for are people who will take reasonably good care of the premises, pay their rent on time, and not be nuisances. Bear in mind that you are about to develop a long-term business relationship with these people, and you don't need the headaches associated with people who won't or can't pay their rent on time. Once a tenant has gained possession and decides not to pay his or her rent and you want that tenant removed, you must do it in such a way that the tenant receives due process of law. Bear in mind that actions to evict a deadbeat will only bring a judgment for rent monies, court costs, and moving fees; and that court cases usually require 30 days or more to litigate. The costs involved, plus additional loss of rent, can be very expensive to an owner when this professional deadbeat moves in to your property. The best way to avoid this catastrophe is to check on your prospect's history-of-paying habits. Telephone a local credit agency and find out what they require to do a credit check for you. If the prospect has no credit, inquire into his or her rent-paying habits with the past two landlords. Occasionally, I will ask prospective tenants if I may see their credit cards. If in fact they have active Visa or MasterCard accounts, that is usually a sign of good credit, so I need not check into it any further. Be sure you check the expiration date when you're examining credit cards.

Your next concern is whether your future tenants will properly care for your investment while they're living in it. About the only way you can determine that is by calling the previous landlord and inquiring into their living habits. Incidentally, in my 20 years of landlording experience, I have observed certain habits of human nature. I have noticed that people who take good care of their car will, in most cases, take good care of their home. Conversely, people who drive a dirty, ill-maintained car almost invariably have dirty and messy homes, and won't take very good care of your property. This observation also usually holds true for kids. If the children of the family are reasonably well dressed in clean clothes, you can correctly assume that the parents will also take care of other things, such as your investment. So, when your prospective tenants arrive at your available unit, check out the condition of the car and the children, if any. Later, if you have any doubts about renting to the prospects, let your observations assist in making your decision.

Finally, you need to financially qualify your prospects on their ability to pay the rent. Guidelines for rent qualification are as follows: The monthly rent should not exceed 25 percent of the tenant's gross monthly income. However, if the tenant has no consumer debt (i.e., car loans and credit card payments), then he or she can afford up to 33 percent of gross monthly income. Spouse income can be included, but not overtime pay. For example, if your prospect grosses $2000 per month and has some consumer debt, then he or she really cannot afford to pay more than $500 per month in rent ($2000 × 25%). If he or she has no consumer debt, then he or she could afford one-third of $2000, or $667 per month in rent.

Deposits

Generally speaking, the more at risk you are, the more you should require in deposits. You are more at risk when the family to whom you rent has children or pets such as dogs and cats. Usually, the security deposit on an unfurnished unit can be from 75 to 100 percent of the first month's rent. This amount can be adjusted upward for each child or pet in the family. A security deposit is a refundable deposit. Any damage done by the tenants, if any, is deducted from the deposit, then sent to them within 30 days of their moving out.

Another necessary deposit is the nonrefundable cleaning deposit. The cleaning deposit is normally $75 to $125, depending on the size and value of the rental unit. Before your tenants move in, be sure to inform them that both the security and cleaning deposits cannot be applied to the last month's rent when they vacate the premises, and that the security deposit will be held until after the unit is vacated with proper notice and in reasonably good condition.

Separate refundable deposits should be required for certain keys and key cards (for parking in secured condominium complexes and for tennis courts, etc.). Usually $10 is adequate for keys and $25 each for key cards.

Moving In

Before your tenants move in and become residents in your rental unit, certain items have to be addressed. All monies owed to you have to be paid, in advance, in cash. This includes the first month's rent (or first and last if it's a long-term lease) and all deposits, including security, cleaning, and key deposits. Be sure the rental agreement is signed and that there is a copy available for the tenant. Also be sure the tenant has one set of keys, plus information on whom to call for the turn-on of all utilities. Finally, inform the tenant that you expect the rent to be paid on time, that there is a three-day grace period, but after that a late fee will be charged (See lease provisions in Appendix 2).

Rent Collection

Remember, your investment in real estate is purely a money-making enterprise, not a downtown charity mission. Investors who yield to delinquent or nonpaying deadbeats are courting financial disaster. Therefore, be firm with your collection policies and inform your new tenants, at the time they move in, what you expect of them. However, you can be flexible; all rents do not have to be paid on the first day of the month. Under certain circumstances, some people might receive their paychecks on the tenth of the month or the fifteenth. If this is the case, make their rent due on a date that coincides with their payday.

After all move-in fees have been paid in cash, you can then allow checks for monthly rent payments. This policy is fine, unless you receive a bad check; once you do, accept only cash or money orders from the individual from that point on. Check bouncers are a habitual bunch. If you continue to accept checks after one has bounced, you can be assured that more rubber checks will eventually bounce through your bank account.

Rent checks should be mailed directly to an address of your choice. Once a tenant has established a good payment history with you, more lenient allowances can be made when unforeseen circumstances occur, such as loss of employment, illness, or death in the family. Whatever the case, definite commitments must be made as to when the debt will be paid, and the matter must immediately be followed up if the debt is not paid.

Resident Manager; Rent Collection Policy

The following are recommended procedures in the event you have a resident manager living in your multi-unit building. Rent collection should always be in the form of checks or money orders. Absolutely no cash should be accepted. (An exception can be made in an emergency or when someone is extremely late in paying the rent.) By having a policy of accepting only checks or money orders, you will eliminate any temptation of the resident manager to borrow small amounts of cash, and you will alleviate the risk of the rent monies being stolen.

Each month's rent receipts can be deposited by the resident manager. To facilitate this, order a rubber stamp; the manager can stamp the back of the rent checks ("For Deposit Only" . . .) and deposit them in your bank account.

Receipt of rent is occasionally requested by the tenant. Therefore, give the manager a receipt pad in triplicate. One copy of the rent receipt can then be available for the tenant, one for the manager, and one for the owner's records.

Eviction Procedure (Nonpayment of Rent)

The following procedure is common in most states for the lawful eviction of a tenant for nonpayment of rent:

1. The tenant in default is served with a Three-Day Notice to Pay Rent or Quit the Premises. The person serving the notice should be a marshal—not the landlord, owner, or resident manager—in order to ensure proper legal procedure.
2. An Unlawful Detainer is filed with the municipal court clerk, and a Summons is issued.
3. The tenant is served with a Summons and a Complaint.
4. The tenant has the legal right to answer the Complaint and plead his case. In that event, a trial is held.
5. The default of the tenant is taken (if there is no trial) and given to the owner.
6. The court issues a Writ of Possession.
7. The marshal receives the Writ of Possession.
8. The marshal evicts the tenant.

BUDGETING

Your successful operation of a rental building will ultimately depend on your carefully planning a budget, and then sticking to it without exception. A budget is basically a financial plan for upcoming years. Projections of all income and expenses are made so that you can have an overall view of the building's financial well-being. If owners do not properly plan income and expenses, the ultimate disaster of financial suicide is inevitable. Over the years, allocations for certain replacement items have to be budgeted and paid for when they need replacing. What happens when owners do not plan properly is deferred maintenance. That, in turn, causes vacancies; vacancies, in turn, cause loss of income, further deferred maintenance, and eventual loss in value.

Good budgeting not only encompasses the planning of income and expenses but also the future replacement of capital items such as carpeting, roofs, pool equipment, and furniture. These items are very costly, but through properly planned budgets they can easily be replaced when necessary. Thus, a contingency fund should be set aside and held in reserve for this purpose. For example, carpeting usually has to be replaced every seven years, on average. As of this writing, new carpeting for a one-bedroom apartment costs about $700 and will last for seven years. Therefore, $100 per year per apartment (about $8 per month) should be set aside in a contingency fund to replace carpeting. Similarly, a replacement reserve fund must be set up for items such as draperies, roofing, furniture, and appliances.

The best way to budget these items is to estimate total outlay for all future capital expenditures, maintaining contingency funds for each item in a savings account to use when the money is required. For example, let's say you determine that the cost of a new roof is $1200, and that it will last for 20 years. You divide the total cost by the total number of months and the result is the amount that should be budgeted each month ($1200 divided by 240 months = $5 per month allocation for a replacement reserve for roofing).

Expense items, such as property taxes and hazard insurance, also have to be budgeted. (Note: Taxes and insurance frequently are paid out of an impound account which is already part of your monthly loan payment. If this is the case, it won't be necessary for you to pay the taxes and insurance premium separately, because the holder of the first mortgage will pay them from the impound account. If the first note holder is not paying the taxes and insurance, then it will be necessary for you to include these items in your budget.) Property taxes are projected at 1/12 of the annual tax bill per month. Be sure to allow for a future increase by the assessor. Hazard insurance is likewise 1/12 of the annual insurance premium.

As a rule of thumb, 5 percent of gross collected rents is usually an adequate amount to be budgeted for replacement reserves. However, this amount would have to be increased if your building has additional equipment such as an elevator, heated pool, or jacuzzi.

KEEPING RECORDS

Proper record-keeping procedures are necessary, so that the information will be accessible when needed (especially when income tax time arrives or in the event the IRS decides to make an untimely audit). Keeping records can be accomplished very simply when your investments are single-family homes. All you need is a separate 8.5" × 11" manila envelope, properly labeled, for each home; you keep all records and expense items inside the envelope. Note all collected income on the outside of the envelope, along with addresses of note holders, balance owing on the notes, and initial cost of the property. At the end of each year, start a new envelope for the upcoming year.

Multi-unit buildings require a little more elaborate record-keeping system, with a separate set of records for each building. Make up file folders and label them "General Records," "Tenant Records," and "Receipts and Expenses." In General Records, retain such information as escrow papers, insurance policies, taxes, notes, and deeds. In Tenant Records, keep all rental applications, rental agreements, and any other data pertaining to your tenants. All tenant information should be kept for credit-rating purposes and landlord inquiries for at least one year after the tenants move out. In Receipts and Expenses, retain receipts for all expenses related to the building and a copy of all rent receipts. Later the expense items can be arranged chronologically for tax purposes. At the end of the tax year, this envelope should be stored separately for at least five years, in case the IRS decides to audit.

Tenant Record Card

A tenant record car is a 5.5" × 8" card used by the owner or manager. Whenever a tenant makes a payment, it is recorded on the Tenant Record Card. (See sample in Appendix 2.)

Journals of Income, Expenses, and Payments

For each multi-unit building, keep a separate journal in which you will post all relevant monthly income and expense data.

It should include sections on income, expenses, loans, and depreciation; it allows you ready access to all current data relating to income and expenses. The first section should record rental and laundry income for each unit for the entire year, and the second section is for posting expenses. All those receipts you have been keeping in a file folder are recorded here monthly. Anything for which you do not have receipts can be recorded from your checking account record. Examples of the monthly Journal of Income and Expenses and Payment Record follow (Figures 11.1 and 11.2).

Once you have completed an entire page on the Expense and Payment Record, total each column and bring the balance forward to the next sheet; then start posting your latest entries. After you have posted your last expenditure for the year, total the last sheet and you'll have your annual expenses for each category of your building.

Be careful not to post on your expense record such capital items as carpeting or a new roof. These are depreciable items, not expenses.

Monthly Income Record   Page # _____

Address _____

Year _____

Unit	Jan	Feb	Mar	Apr	May	Jun	Jul	Aug	Sep	Oct	Nov	Dec
1	400	400	400	400	400							
2	390	390	390	390	390							
3	425	425	425	425	425							
4	275	275	275	275	275							
5	415	415	415	415	415							
6	460	460	460	460	460							
7												
8												
Tot.	2365	2365	2365	2365	2365							

Figure 11.1 Monthly Income Record

Expense and Payment Record

Address _____ Year _____ Page # _____

Date	Paid To	Paid For	Total Paid	Mortgage Principal	Mortgage Interest	Tax	Ins	Mgt	Repairs & Maint.
1. 1/1	bank	1st mort	760	122.80	427.20	120	90		
2. 1/1	Smith	2nd	125	92.40	32.60				
3. 1/3	hdwr.	pts.	9.60						
4. 1/7	water	water	56.71						
5. 1/8	muni ct	evict	21						
6. 2/1	bank	1st mort	760	124.06	425.94	120	90		
7.									

Figure 11.2 Expense and Payment Record

Depreciation Records

Depreciable items are property or equipment having an extended useful life and considered to be improvements to the property. Some examples are carpeting, elevators, new linoleum, roof replacement, swimming pool. Each of these or similar items must be depreciated on a separate depreciation record form, such as is shown in Figure 11.3. (See also depreciation methods, Chapter 10.)

Annual Statement of Income

This statement (Figure 11.4 is an example of one) brings together all relative income and expenses for the year and shows the net profit or loss. Notice how depreciation, not an out-of-pocket expense, is deducted last for tax purposes. (This is the actual "tax-shelter" benefit of owning income-producing real estate.) The bottom line is the net profit or loss given to the Internal Revenue Service.

Figure 11.3 Location and Description of Capital Improvement: 3750 Raymond LA, CA. A 19-Unit Apartment Building

Date acquired:	Jan. 1987
New or Used:	Used
Cost or value:	$220,000
Land value:	40,000
Salvage value:	0
Depreciable Basis:	$180,000
Method of depreciation:	straight line
Useful life:	27.5 years

	Year	Prior Deprec.	Deprec. Balance	% Year Held	Deprec. this yr.
1.	1987	0	180,000	100	6,545
2.	1988		173,455	100	6,545
3.	1989		166,910	100	6,545
4.					

Figure 11.4 Annual Statement of Income Example Location: 3750 Raymond, LA, CA. Year: 1968

Income		
Rent	$28,471	
Other (laundry)	629	
Total income	29,100	$29,100
Expenses		
Interest	8,410	
Taxes	4,800	
Utilities	1,812	
Service, repairs	321	
Pest control	120	
Insurance	850	
Management	1,800	
Total Expenses	18,113	18,113
Net Income (before depreciation)		10,987
Less depreciation		−6,545
Net Income (or loss) for tax purposes		4,442

REPAIRS

Part of the "no-hassle" management theory is to avoid some of the nuisances common to managing residential rentals. Commercial landlords solved the "who is responsible for certain repairs" problem by making the tenants responsible for paying for repairs up to a certain limit. In this way, the landlord doesn't have to get involved with certain minor repairs.

In the sample Rental Agreement (located in Appendix 2) you'll find a clause under Repairs, which I refer to as the "no-hassle repair clause." It states that the tenant is responsible for the first $100 in repairs on the rented property. In other words, if a window breaks, the plumbing stops up, or the washer breaks down, the tenant pays the repair bill, up to $100. By making the tenant responsible for certain repairs, the landlord is spared having to make troublesome phone calls requesting repairs.

One more point about the no-hassle repair clause: At the time of move-in, be sure to inform your tenants of your repair policy, and give them the phone number of a competent repair person.

Points to Remember

Property management can be a truly rewarding experience or it can be a burdensome daily chore. I have offered you a concise, yet thorough, guide for total property management to assist you in making decisions and to help you avoid costly pitfalls. Foremost among these guidelines is properly screening your prospective tenants, thereby helping to ensure that you will have good-paying tenants who will properly care for your investment. Don't forget the importance of the "no-hassle" clause written into your rental agreement; this will eliminate 90 percent of the late-night phone calls by your tenants requesting repairs. These simple procedures will help to make your investment a truly efficient, successful, and profitable experience.

PART FOUR
How to Tap Retirement Income from Home Equity

12 INTRODUCTION TO THE POSSIBILITIES

Introducing . . . an in-depth look at how to profitably tap retirement income from the value in your home. You have several alternatives, and what's best depends primarily on whether you need to raise money from your home, and how much.

The primary alternative we'll discuss is trading-down, which means selling the large, expensive home and buying or renting a smaller, less expensive one. But which is better, renting or buying the replacement home? You also have several possible methods of selling the big, expensive home. Do you sell for cash, or is it better to carry back an interest-bearing note? In addition, depending on your cash needs, you could also rent it out with a Buy-Option. Should you?

The purpose of the trade-down is to allow you a certain amount of financial freedom. Trading the big, expensive house for a smaller home substantially reduces your living costs. You save on property taxes, insurance premiums, and maintenance costs. But more importantly, the trade-down also offers you income.

Besides trading-down, you have several other options. How about staying put and taking out a mortgage that pays you tax-free income? You could take out a home equity loan, a reverse annuity mortgage, or a sale-leaseback.

It's likely that your overall living expenses will probably be one-third less than your pre-retirement costs. If your expected income from investments, Social Security, pensions, and other sources falls short of your requirements, then you may have no other option but to tap your prime asset.

In most cases, you'll probably find that selling out and buying or renting a smaller home is likely to be the smartest alternative. Nevertheless, let's explore all the possibilities to determine the bottom-line result of each.

TRADING-DOWN

As mentioned before, trading-down is selling the large, expensive home in order to buy or rent a smaller, less expensive one. The trade-down has the following advantages: It reduces monthly living costs such as property taxes, maintenance, insurance premiums, and mortgage payments, if any; you receive cash or income from the sale of the larger home; and, if you meet certain age and residency requirements, you can avoid tax on $125,000 in profits from the sale. (See Chapter 10 for more tax details.)

Essentially, when trading-down you have four alternatives for the disposition of the large, expensive home. They are: 1) to sell it outright and receive all cash for your equity; 2) to sell it on installment by accepting a down payment and carrying back an interest-bearing note for the balance owing; 3) to rent it with a Buy-Option; or 4) to simply rent it. The alternative that's best for you depends greatly on whether you need to raise money—and how much. Now let's look at each alternative in detail.

Sell It Outright and Receive All Cash

Being totally cashed out of this property has only one primary advantage. It is that you immediately realize the profit after the sale, which means you'll have plenty of ready cash available. But this is only an advantage if you have a good place in which to reinvest the proceeds.

Realistically, if you sold for cash and invested the proceeds conservatively, such as in certificates of deposit, you could expect a yield of about 8 percent in today's market. If you don't need the cash, then you could do a lot better than 8 percent by considering the other alternatives.

When you do sell, be sure to time the sale to take advantage of available tax benefits. If you or your spouse is age 55 or older and has lived in the home for at least three of the five years preceding the sale, you can exclude from taxes up to $125,000 of the gain realized on the sale. Should the gain exceed $125,000, you can defer tax on the excess by reinvesting the money, within two years, in a new residence; however, the new residence must be of equal or greater value than the home you sold.

Sell on Installment

Selling the big, expensive home on installment is only practical if the following two conditions exist: 1) If you don't need the cash and prefer income from the sale; and 2) the installment sale requires that all existing underlying loans on the property are assumable. (Without assumable loans the buyer is required to pay all cash, or to originate a new loan to purchase your home.)

If you're already cash-rich, then consider an installment sale which, at current rates, offers you 10 to 11 percent on the loan you carry back on the sale of your residence. This return is greater than what you could expect from certain other sources. Conservative investing in Treasury Bills or CDs yields only about 8 percent in today's market. Yet you could earn 10 to 11 percent by financing the sale of your home, which, incidentally, is security for the note. (If the borrower defaults on your note, you have the right to foreclose on the property in order to protect your interest.)

Therefore, if you need the cash to retire on, or to buy another home, then it's likely that cashing out would be advisable. On the other hand, if you don't need the cash, consider the secured earnings that an installment sale offers.

Rent with Buy-Option

Besides selling outright or on installment, consider renting the property and giving the tenants an option to buy it. This way, instead of just collecting rent, you can also collect an additional option fee which applies toward the purchase price.

This method would be practical if you don't need the cash from the sale of the home, and if you intend to live in the area of the optioned property. (For more details on the Buy-Option, see Chapter 5.)

Renting

Renting the property would be the least advantageous method for the disposition of your property. You wouldn't receive nearly as much income from the property as you would under the other three methods, although renting it could be advantageous if you expect the house to appreciate substantially in the future.

Table 12.1 shows four alternatives available to a retiring couple in the disposition of a mortgage-free house worth $200,000.

Table 12.1 shows us that if the couple sells outright for all cash, they can invest the proceeds in CDs earning 8 percent which yield $14,800 annually. They'd also have $186,000 in principal available, should they need it later.

If the couple arranges an installment sale, they'd receive $30,000 for a down payment which is invested in CDs earning 8 percent. They'd also earn $20,367 annually on the $170,000 note from the buyer, a note which pays 10.5 percent principal and interest for 20 years.

If the couple rents the house with a Buy-Option, they'll receive $1600 per month rent, of which $400 applies to the purchase price. However, they'd still have to pay property taxes and insurance until the Buy-Option is exercised.

If the couple simply rents the house, they'll receive $1200 per month rent, which results in $14,400 annually in gross income. However, similar to the Buy-Option, they'd still have to pay property taxes and insurance.

Based on the comparison of the four alternatives available, the couple will receive the most annual income by selling the house on installment. Primarily this is because the couple would earn 2.5 percent more in yield than if they sold the property outright and earned 8 percent in CDs.

Table 12.1 Disposition of $200,000 Mortgage-free House.

Alternative Used	Proceeds from sale	Proceed's annual earnings in 8% CDs	Property taxes & ins.	Mortgage or rental income from house	Total annual earnings
Sell outright	$186,000	$14,880	–0–	–0–	$14,880
Installment sale	$30,000	$2,400	–0–	$20,367	$22,767
Rent with Buy-option	–0–	–0–	*$2,400	$19,200	$19,200
Renting	–0–	–0–	$2,400	$14,400	$14,400

*After Buy-option is exercised, the buyer will pay property taxes and insurance.

BUYING VERSUS RENTING

After you've solved the disposition of the big, expensive home under the trade-down alternative, you have to decide either to buy or rent a replacement home. Your decision will depend on a number of things.

Buying a home offers you interest and property tax deduction benefits, and the possibility of property appreciation. Renting a home means no down payment or closing costs, more mobility, and no hassles involved with selling the property.

Should You Pay All Cash or Finance the Replacement Home?

If the retired home buyer can afford to pay all cash for the replacement home, should he or she do so? No. The primary reason retirees should not pay all cash for a retirement home is that once they tie up their money, they usually can't quickly borrow that much money again for emergencies or investment opportunities.

Retirees are often unable to borrow money, except at excessive rates of interest. The time to borrow money is when you're in good health and have adequate income, not when you need the money. When retirees buy, they should always take the maximum home loan available with the minimum cash down payment.

Why Renting is Better

Unless you're already familiar with real estate values in the area to which you move, or you've invested in a vacation home during your working years, you're better off renting at first. This is because, in most cases, people tend to retire in areas where they've previously vacationed; they like the area, but probably vacationed at a resort hotel in the area; by doing so, they never really became familiar with the community nor the real estate values.

Renting also allows you more mobility, especially under a month-to-month rental agreement. This way, if you decide to travel over an extended period you can simply put the furniture in storage and take off, without having to pay rent or worry about an unattended home.

Also, renting doesn't require large amounts of cash, which you'll need if you decide to purchase a retirement home.

What about a recreational vehicle (RV) for a retirement home? Before going ahead with such a decision, rent one for a month and try it out. A first class RV, along with all the extras, licensing, and insurance, is a major investment. Once a new one leaves the showroom, it loses 25 percent of its value.

Now let's look at alternative methods of converting home equity into retirement income.

13 ALTERNATIVE METHODS FOR TAPPING EQUITY FROM THE VALUE IN YOUR HOME

For those of you who prefer not to sell the house, there are four methods available for deriving income from the value in your home. They are: 1) a reverse annuity mortgage; 2) a home equity loan or refinancing; 3) a sale-leaseback; and 4) renting out an accessory room.

About three out of four Americans over 65 own their homes, with more than $50,000 in equity waiting to be tapped. The easiest way to use this equity would be to take out a home equity loan; however, most retirees living on fixed incomes cannot qualify for such a loan. For them, a reverse annuity mortgage (RAM) that pays tax-free income to the borrower could be more appropriate.

REVERSE ANNUITY MORTGAGE (RAM)

A RAM is opposite in function to other types of loans. Under terms of the RAM, the homeowner receives from the lender a monthly payment (annuity) which is applied against equity in the home. Other types of loans offer the homeowner a lump sum; then the homeowner makes payments to the lender until the balance owing is paid off.

The reverse mortgage emerged to assist senior adults on

171

fixed incomes who have substantial equity or own their home free and clear. Instead of selling the home to make use of the equity, homeowners can take out a RAM whereby the lender makes monthly payments to them in the form of an annuity. Here's how it works:

Let's say you own your home free and clear and it's worth $100,000. A lender might agree to lend you up to $80,000, usually at a fixed rate of interest. But instead of receiving the $80,000 in a lump sum, you receive it in monthly install-ments. These installments, or annuities, are in effect tax-free income.

You make no interest payments on the RAM. All principal and compounded interest, complete with typical closing costs of 2.5 percent of the borrowed amount, is due and payable at the end of the loan's term. At that point, the house has to be sold to pay off the reverse mortgage, which includes principal and accumulated interest. In addition, the lender's fee could also include a portion of the property's appreciation. If you die before the term of the RAM expires, then your estate pays off the loan.

INDIVIDUAL RETIREMENT
MORTGAGE ACCOUNT (IRMA)

In some parts of the country, another kind of reverse mortgage is available. If the homeowner is 62 or older, under terms of the IRMA he or she receives monthly income for as long as he or she lives. The loan matures either upon the sale of the home or the death of the homeowner or surviving spouse. In other words, the homeowner may never have to repay the loan. In-stead, the loan will be repaid by the surviving estate.

Terms of the IRMA can allow the homeowner to retain some portion of the home's value for himself or herself or for his or her heirs. Thus, not all the home's equity need be used.

Monthly income from the IRMA is tax-free. The amount of monthly advances is determined by the age of the borrower and the appraised value of the property (you can usually bor-row up to 80 percent of the equity in the house).

The IRMA could be a bargain if you outlive your acturarial life expectancy, yet a short term IRMA is a considerable risk. The loan cost could outweigh the benefits it provides during your lifetime. If you die soon after arranging the IRMA, your estate must repay the lender all of the monthly advances you received, with interest, plus all or part of the home's appreciation since the mortgage was signed.

Reverse Mortgage Conclusions

Before going ahead with a reverse mortgage, consider the following:

* Avoid reverse mortgages that allow the lender to share in the appreciation of the home. Lenders earn enough in interest charges and closing costs without taking all or part of the appreciation earned on your home.
* How long do you intend to live in the house? If you plan to move within five years, the costs of a RAM will be exorbitant.
* Do you have children or other heirs to consider? Remember that the repayment of the RAM may come out of your estate. You can retain some equity in your house by exempting a portion of its value from the loan transaction. However, you'll have to settle for reduced annuity payments from the lender.

REFINANCING VERSUS A HOME EQUITY LOAN

If you own your home free and clear of any existing loans, then refinancing it with a new first mortgage is the obvious choice for tapping your prime asset. You can borrow up to 80 percent of the home's value at a reasonable fixed rate of interest.

On the other hand, if you have an existing underlying loan on the property, then you should carefully consider how you plan to borrow against the equity. You can earn substantial savings depending on the type of financing you choose.

If you have an existing underlying loan on the property, you essentially have two choices: 1) Refinance your existing loan, or 2) take out a second mortgage and leave intact the existing first mortgage in order to make use of the equity in the home. Here is a comparison of the two methods.

The decision either to refinance or to take out a second loan confronts many homeowners who have owned their home several years and would like to spend some of that accumulated equity. In most cases, the existing mortgage loan is at an interest rate below the current prevailing rate of new mortgages. If this is the case, it would be unwise to refinance, because you would be eliminating the value of the existing low-interest loan by replacing it with a costlier, high-interest rate loan. However, it *would* be wise to refinance if the prevailing mortgage loan rate is 2 points or more below the rate that you're already paying on the first mortgage. Usually, a savings of 2 points or more is required to overcome all the costs of initiating a new loan.

Instead of refinancing, you also have the option of taking out a second mortgage loan in order to maintain the value of the present low interest rate on the existing first loan. Let us use as an example a home bought six years ago for $50,000 with a first mortgage attached at 8 percent for a term of 30 years. Payment for principal and interest is $300 a month, and the remaining loan balance after six years of ownership is approximately $38,000. Since the current market value of the house is $80,000, you therefore have about $42,000 equity in the home.

If you refinance the house at an 11.5 percent rate of interest, the lender would advance 80 percent of the market value, of which advance $38,000 must be applied toward paying off the first mortgage loan. Consequently, there would be $26,000 in net proceeds ($80,000 × 80% = $64,000 − $38,000 = $26,000). The new first loan would require monthly payments of $634 to amortize principal and interest over the 30-year term.

On the other hand, if you arranged a second mortgage for an amount of net proceeds equal to that of refinancing, which is $26,000, in today's market the lender would charge you 13.5

Table 13.1 Comparing Refinancing To a Take-Out Second Mortgage

REFINANCING

Amount of net proceeds	Payment on 1st loan	Term of loan	Total amount paid over term of loan
$26,000	$634	30 yrs	$228,240

TAKING OUT A SECOND MORTGAGE

Amount of net proceeds	Payment on 1st	Term remaining on 1st	Payment on 2nd	Term remaining on 2nd	Total amount paid over term
$26,000	$300	25 yrs.	$338	15 yrs.	$150,840

percent. The term of the new second loan would be 15 years with a monthly payment of $338. The total monthly payments of both first and second loans for the next 15 years would be $638 ($338 + $300). After 15 years the second loan would be paid in full, so only a monthly payment of $300 on the existing first mortgage would be required (See Table 13.1).

As Table 13.1 shows, the difference paid over the entire term of the loan is a substantial savings of $77,400 when taking out a second mortgage instead of refinancing. In this particular situation, the property was refinanced at 3.5 points above the rate of the existing loan, and $38,000 went to pay off the original amount owing. This is the primary reason that refinancing costs so much more than the take-out second loan. In addition, although the new take-out second loan interest rate appears high at 13.5 percent, the term is short at 15 years, meaning a substantial savings in the amount of interest because of the short term of the loan.

SALE-LEASEBACK

The sale-leaseback entails selling your home to an investor, then leasing it back from the investor. Likely investor candidates would be your children or other family members.

With a sale-leaseback, the seller generally receives a 10 to 20 percent down payment and a 20-year interest-bearing mortgage. The buyer pays the cost of property taxes, insurance, and maintenance.

A sale-leaseback arrangement with a 10 percent down payment and a 20 year mortgage at 10.5 percent on a $200,000 house could generate $22,844 in income to the seller, who would pay about $18,000 in rent during the first year.

Other than children or other family members, it's frequently difficult to find a sale-leaseback investor who can afford to make the investment.

RENT AN ACCESSORY ROOM

With the kids grown up and probably out on their own, consider renting out a vacant room to a tenant. Depending on the size of the rental and the amenities you offer, you could earn anywhere from $250 to $400 monthly.

Your privacy is dependent on whether the rental unit has a separate bathroom and kitchen. If it doesn't, you'll have to allow the boarder use of a common area which has such facilities.

Also, consider converting the garage to a rental unit.

Converting the Garage to a Rental

In many middle-class neighborhoods, you'll often find an attached garage converted to a rental unit. However, be cautious before doing this, because you could be seriously inhibiting the saleability of the house.

At first glance it appears such a conversion could be lucrative. A converted two-car garage could rent as a studio apartment for about $300 per month. Renovations would entail removing the garage door, installing an entry door, and building a wall. Carpeting would be needed, plus a bathroom and a small kitchen area. Of course, a conversion of this type would be more feasible and economical if the garage walls were already finished and there were existing plumbing lines in the vicinity of the garage.

Total cost would probably be in the range of $3500, which

would be returned to you within one year through rental income. That's the good news. The bad news is that if you go ahead with such a conversion, you obviously no longer have a garage, which could inhibit the sale of the house. This is because most home buyers want a garage; it's a great place to store the cars or other items, and it's an ideal place for a handy person to have a workshop.

You should only consider such a conversion when a storage facility isn't needed, and when you plan to occupy the converted house over a long term. Remember that if you plan to eventually sell the house, most homebuyers would prefer a garage to a rental unit.

14 FINAL COMPARISON OF ALL THE ALTERNATIVES

Now we can take a closer look at each alternative and determine which one is best for you. As a review, the alternatives are:

- Trade-down: Sell for all cash and buy a replacement home
- Trade-down: Sell for all cash and rent a replacement home
- Trade-down: Sell on installment and buy a replacement home
- Trade-down: Sell on installment and rent a replacement home
- Stay in the home and take out a reverse mortgage
- Stay in the home and do nothing
- Stay in the home under a sale-leaseback
- Rent out a room

The following tables illustrate the options available to a retiring couple who own a mortgage-free house worth $200,000. Please note that annual housing costs increase 3 percent annually. Also note that the principal and home equity column shows a gradual increase, which is the result of 6 percent annual appreciation and equity build-up as the mortgage pays down. (In the installment sale tables note that principal on the sold home is being paid down while the couple uses the additional income as living expenses.)

Table 14.1 Trade Down: All-Cash Sale & Buy Home

Year	Additional income	Annual housing cost	Principal & home equity
1	$14,080	$12,000	$186,000
5	14,080	14,040	228,733
10	14,080	16,427	288,935
15	14,080	19,220	374,346

Using this alternative given in Table 14.1, our retirees sell the house for all cash and buy a smaller house for $100,000 with 10 percent down and finance the balance for 20 years at a 10.25 percent fixed rate. They invest the remaining balance of $176,000 ($200,000 less closing costs and down payment) in one-year insured CDs, in this case yielding 8 percent.

In Table 14.2, our retirees sell the house for all cash and rent a replacement house for $800 monthly. Then they invest the remaining $186,000 (selling price less closing costs) in one-year insured CDs, in this case yielding 8 percent.

In Table 14.3, they sell the house on installment, accepting a 10 percent down payment and carrying back a 10.5 percent interest-bearing note on the balance owing for 20 years. They buy a smaller house for $100,000 with 10 percent down and finance the balance for 20 years at 10.25 percent fixed rate. Of the down payment money they receive, they invest $16,000 in insured one-year CDs yielding 8 percent.

Please note that the couple can earn more in interest when selling the house on installment (10.5 percent versus 10.25

Table 14.2 Trade-Down: All-Cash Sale & Rent Home

Year	Additional income	Annual housing costs	Home equity & principal
1	$14,880	$ 9,600	$186,000
5	14,880	11,040	186,000
10	14,880	12,480	186,000
15	14,880	13,920	186,000

Table 14.3 Trade-Down: Installment Sale & Buy Replacement Home

Year	Additional income	Annual housing cost	Principal & home equity
1	$22,844	$12,000	$186,000
5	22,844	14,040	211,273
10	22,844	16,427	242,135
15	22,844	19,220	277,866

percent) because the buyer doesn't have to pay loan origination fees.

In Table 14.4, they sell the house on installment accepting a
10 percent down payment and carry back a 10.5 percent interest bearing note on the balance owing for 20 years. They rent
a smaller house for $800 monthly; the rent then increases 3
percent annually. The down payment money received is invested in CDs yielding 8 percent. Note that the home equity
and principal amount gradually decreases each year as the
note pays down and the couple spends the income on living
costs.

Using the alternative in Table 14.5, the couple can take out
a reverse annuity mortgage that pays them $662 monthly. At
the end of the 15-year term, they will have to sell the house to
repay the loan.

In Table 14.6, the couple stays put and leaves their equity
intact, they'll maintain the full value of their property. In this
example, the house appreciates 6 percent annually. However,
the couple will need income from other sources to meet rising
costs such as property taxes, insurance, and maintenance.

In Table 14.7, the couple chooses a sale-leaseback, they sell
the house on installment, then lease it back from the buyer.
The sellers accept a 10 percent down payment and carry back
an interest-bearing note at 10.5 percent on the balance owing
for 20 years. They lease-back the home for $1500 per month
(this sum increases 3 percent annually). Of the down payment
money received, $16,000 is invested in CDs yielding 8 per-
cent. Please note that the amounts in the principal column
continually decline as the interest-bearing note pays down. At
the end of 20 years the note will have a zero balance.

Table 14.4 Trade-Down: Installment Sale & Rent Replacement Home

Year	Additional income	Annual housing costs	Home equity & principal
1	$22,844	$ 9,600	$186,000
5	22,844	11,040	168,540
10	22,844	12,480	139,200
15	22,844	13,920	89,520

Table 14.5 Reverse Mortgage

Year	Additional income	Annual Housing costs	Home equity & principal
1	$7,944	$4,800	$176,650
5	7,944	5,616	146,234
10	7,944	6,571	85,583
15	7,944	7,688	–0–

Table 14.6 Do Nothing

Year	Additional income	Annual Housing costs	Home equity & principal
1	–0–	$4,800	$200,000
5	–0–	5,616	267,645
10	–0–	6,571	358,169
15	–0–	7,688	479,311

Table 14.7 Sale-Leaseback

Year	Additional income	Annual housing costs	Principal
1	$22,844	$18,000	$200,000
5	22,844	20,700	162,540
10	22,844	23,805	133,200
15	22,844	27,376	83,520

Table 14.8 Conclusions

Alternative used	A Additional income	B Annual housing costs	Difference between A & B
Trade-down: All-cash sale & buy home	$14,080	$12,000	+$2,080
Trade-down: All-cash sale & rent home	14,880	9,600	+5,280
Trade-down: Installment sale & buy home	22,844	12,000	+10,844
Trade-down: Installment sale & rent home	22,844	9,600	+13,244
Reverse mortgage: stay put	7,944	4,800	+ 3,144
Do nothing and stay put	–0–	4,800	– 4,800
Sale-leaseback and stay put	22,844	18,000	+ 4,844
Rent out a room and stay put	4,800	4,800	–0–

CONCLUSIONS

Table 14.8 illustrates, for each alternative, the difference in surplus income between first-year annual housing cost and additional income.

As you can see, after comparing all the alternatives, *the best alternative is to trade-down, using the installment sale, and rent the replacement home.* This course of action not only provides the retirees with more additional income, it also gives them more surplus income than do the other alternatives.

Staying in the home and doing nothing is the worst alternative, because in our example it produces negative income of $4800 annually.

15 HOW TO SELL
YOUR PROPERTY

Throughout the United States, two-thirds of residential real estate is sold using the services of a broker; the remainder is sold by individual owners. The broker's fee for selling your home is usually six percent of the selling price. In return, the broker assists you in determining the right selling price, shows the home to prospective buyers, and lists it with the Multiple Listing Service (MLS). Listing with the MLS substantially enlarges the market for potential buyers, because brokers and agents from other offices are made aware of your listing, and they can then inform their buyers of your available property.

Besides showing the property, the listing agent is also helpful at the closing of the sale. In many cases the broker acts as the liaison between you and the buyer, working out any difficulties that may arise.

However, should you decide to save the sales commission and sell the property yourself, keep in mind that, on average, it takes 87 days to sell a home. This reveals that selling a house is, by no means, an easy task. Much preparation is required to do the job right. If you're prepared to invest the time and effort necessary to sell your own property and save the six percent commission, go right ahead. The following material is a step-by-step guide to accomplishing this.

TIMING THE SALE

Traditionally, there are good times during the year to sell residential property, as well as good times to buy. Good times to sell are during the spring and fall, primarily because it's then that most buyers are looking for property (especially if they have children attending school). Probably the worst time of the year to sell residential property is during the winter, especially around Christmas. During the holiday times, potential buyers are usually too preoccupied with other things to concern themselves with buying a home. Conversely, since during this time there is a deficiency of buyers, it's the best time to make your purchase.

PRICE IT RIGHT

To establish the right price, it's first necessary to establish the least price you'll accept. Then you can adjust your price upward from this point, allowing a little room for price negotiations. Most buyers like to negotiate, so allow yourself a little flexibility.

NECESSARY DOCUMENTS AND INFORMATION

After deciding what price to ask for the property, begin gathering the documents and information you'll need to consummate the sale.

You will need the following information from the loan documents:

- Is there a prepayment penalty on the first mortgage and, if so, will the lender waive it if the buyer obtains his mortgage from the same lender?
- What is the current principal balance owing on the loan?
- Is there a tax and insurance impound account and, if so, what is the balance in that account?

Note that the prepayment penalty is a cost to you, levied by the lender according to the original loan agreement, charging you a penalty (six months' interest on the unpaid balance is common) for repaying the loan before it's due. This penalty covers the lender's cost in reclaiming, and then reloaning, the money which you paid back prematurely. It may be waived.

You will also need copies of the following documents:

- The paid tax receipt for the previous year.
- The survey of your property.
- Evidence of title.

HOME SELLING TIPS

Whether or not you use the services of a broker, it is necessary to prepare the entire property for its eventual sale. The following material is a guide to preparation in order to get a quick and bona fide offer for your property.

When showing homes to prospective buyers, realtors often say "this property has good curb appeal" (looks appealing at first sight) or "this house shows well." This descriptive jargon is relevant to selling, because in order to get the best price for your home it's wise to prepare it so that it looks its best.

Unless you want to sell a fixer-upper, or one that looks like a fixer-upper, you should put your house (and the surrounding grounds) in order, so as to get the most out of it. Some of the preparation can simply consist of tidying up around the exterior of the house. But unless you've been an extremely tidy housekeeper, which most of us are not, you'll have to do some minor repair and touch-ups to meet good condition standards. Remember, anything in obvious disrepair will eventually be discounted from the offer price.

First impressions are most important. If the house doesn't look appealing from the curb, the prospective buyer might not consider getting out of the car to look further. The following are suggestions that will get the prospect out of the car and into your home for a further inspection; a quick sale may be the result.

Exterior

Tidy up the exterior grounds by removing any debris, old cars, and so on. Cut the grass and trim the hedges and shrubs. Neatly arrange and organize items such as outdoor furniture and firewood.

Store, or have removed from the property, items such as broken-down dishwashers, water heaters, and water softeners. (Avoid the look of a junkyard.)

Rake the lawn thoroughly and sweep the sidewalk and driveway.

Tour the perimeter of your property; repair any broken fencing, and paint or stain areas that need attention.

Carefully inspect your front door. It's one of the first items your home-hunting prospects will examine. If it shows signs of wear, give it a fresh coat of paint or stain. While you're at it, spruce up the house numbers with a touch-up paint job, or replace them with new shiny brass numbers.

Quite often, repainting the entire exterior of the house isn't necessary; instead, you can substantially improve the appearance simply by repainting all the trim.

Repair any broken windows or screens, then wash them; They'll look brighter.

Interior

When you're finished with the exterior, start on the interior. The objective here is to make your home look organized, spacious, bright, warm, and comfortable. I can't overemphasize cleanliness. This would be a good time for a thorough spring cleaning. A clean house will sell much faster than a dirty one.

Brighten dull rooms with a fresh coat of white, beige, or antique white paint. Lighter colors make rooms appear bigger and brighter, and neutral colors will go better with the new buyer's furnishings. Instead of taking the time and effort to pull down old wallpaper and put up new, try sprucing up the trim.

Rooms with too much furniture show very poorly. Prospective buyers look for lots of room. Rearrange your furniture to make rooms appear more spacious. Put excessive furniture in storage, then rearrange and organize what's left. You'll be surprised how much unnecessary stuff can accumulate over the years.

General Tips

Have a garage sale to clear out all your unwanted stuff. You can earn extra money, and you won't have to pay the movers to relocate all those unwanted items.

Clean all windows and mirrors. If the carpet is dirty, have it professionally cleaned. If the carpet appears overly worn, consider having it replaced. It's unlikely that you will recover the cost of a new carpet in the sale of your home, but most likely it will sell faster.

Clear your kitchen counters to make the kitchen appear more organized and spacious. Clean and polish all appliances in the kitchen, and make the sink shiny and sparkling.

Clean and shine the tub, toilet, and sink in the bathrooms.

Break out the tool box and start fixing all those little things you've been putting up with for so long. You know what they are: leaky faucet, loose door knobs, cracked receptacle and switch covers. Secure those loose moldings, towel racks, and anything else that wobbles.

These are all little items of disrepair that can detract from the beauty and function of your home. When a prospective buyer begins examining your home during a walk-through, he or she is mentally keeping track of any shortcomings. Too many little things in disrepair will bring a lower offer, if any at all, than if the house were in excellent condition.

When it's finally time to show your home to prospective buyers, all the preparations you made will definitely be worth the effort; your home will receive more and better offers than if you were ill-prepared. But there are a few additional things you should do, just before you show the home, that will add that little extra touch of comfort and hominess.

Just before your prospective buyers arrive, clear out the kids and secure the pets where they won't cause any distraction. Turn off the television and put on some soft music. Turn on all the lights in the house to make it as bright as possible, even during the day. If you have a fireplace, fire it up also. Liven up the aroma in your home with freshly baked cinnamon rolls right out of the oven. Put clean towels on the racks and fresh flowers in a vase. Treat yourself for making your home such a tidy showplace.

When the prospects arrive, make yourself scarce (only when using a broker, that is). Your absence will make potential buyers more at ease. Your presence will only distract them from the job at hand, that of looking over your home and asking questions (that the agent must answer). If you must be there, try to avoid any conversation with the prospects, because the agent needs their full attention to stimulate interest in the features of your home.

Do not complicate the sale of your home by discussing the separate sale of certain appliances or the fact that you wish to keep certain personal items. Personal property, such as furniture and unattached appliances, can be negotiated later, at a more appropriate time.

Always maintain your home in showplace condition, as you never know when just the right prospect might show up. Your agent will usually make appointments with you for showings, but if casual browsers drop in for an unexpected visit, it is best not to show your home. Ask for their name and phone number and refer the information to your agent, if you have one.

Keep in mind that it takes time to sell a home. Be patient. Keep your home on the market for as long as it takes. Selling your home requires a lot of exposure to a lot of prospective buyers.

You might also consider offering a one-year home warranty plan, which would offer a little more value and would overcome questions about the working order of major home systems. These policies, which are available through most national real estate brokerage companies, insures your home for one year against the cost of most major repairs.

PROPERTY INFORMATION SHEET

The Property Information Sheet (Figure 15.1) is necessary only if you plan to sell the property yourself. It's a list of all the vital measurements and other information about your

Address _____ Selling Price $_____
_____

Existing first mortgage balance _____ at _____ %
Existing second mortgage balance _____ at _____ %
Monthly payments on first $ _____ plus taxes and insurance $ _____
Monthly payments on second $_____
Architectural style: _____ Const. _____ Basmt: _____

LR _____	Age: _____	Heat: _____
DR _____	Lot Size: _____	Air cond. _____
Kit _____	Garage: _____	220 Wiring: _____
Dinette: _____	Curbs & gut. _____	Water htr: _____
Fam. rm. _____	Paved st. _____	Water soft: _____
Other rm. _____	Sidewalk: _____	
Bath: _____	Water: _____	
Bath: _____	Sewer: _____	
Bath: _____	Septic: _____	
BR: _____		
BR: _____	Schools: High _____	Grade: _____
BR: _____	Middle _____	
BR: _____		

Draperies and curtains: _____
Carpeting: _____
Items included: Oven _____ Range _____ Frig _____
TV antenna _____ Disposal _____ Dishwasher _____
Items not included: _____
_____
Owner _____ Phone _____

Figure 15.1 Property Information Sheet

home that you'll distribute to prospective buyers. Measure, as
accurately as you can, each room; use a 50-foot (or longer) tape
measure. Enter this and all the other called-for information on
the Property Information Sheet and make copies for distribution.

OPEN HOUSE AND THE FOR-SALE SIGN

Real estate agents hold open house on their listed properties
mostly over weekends, when the majority of potential buyers
have time off from work and can easily go house-hunting.

If you plan to sell your home yourself, weekends would also be the best time to hold your open house. If, by chance, other home-owners are holding open house during the same time as yours, you'll actually benefit from it. Numerous open houses in the same neighborhood mean more prospective buyers will have the opportunity to see your property.

Unless your property is located on a well-traveled thoroughfare, you'll need several open-house signs to direct prospects to your property. Count the number of turns a prospect has to make from a major thoroughfare in order to get to your property. That will be the number of signs you'll need.

Your open-house signs should be 24 inches square with red letters on a white background. Each sign should read OPEN HOUSE with the address at the bottom and a red arrow pointing in the correct direction.

The sign in your front yard should read FOR SALE BY OWNER in red with your phone number below. In addition to the for-sale sign, consider placing small pennants or flags near the street; these are excellent attention-getters for your sale.

ADVERTISING

The purpose of your advertising is to get prospects interested enough in your property to come by and see it for themselves. Place your ad in the classified section of your Sunday newspaper, because Sundays are when realtors place their ads. Prospective buyers are accustomed to looking for homes in the Sunday paper.

In addition, consider placing an ad for your open house in the Sunday paper. Most newspapers have a separate section classified under "Open House."

THE SALES AGREEMENT

At this point your property, both inside and out, is tidy and in complete repair. Your advertisements are running and the phone is ringing off the hook with inquiries. Prospective buyers have been walking through your home day after day, and, finally, somebody says they're interested in buying your home, or that they wish to sit down and discuss terms of a sale at your earliest convenience. What you have now is not a sale, but a serious and interested prospect. Now is the time to negotiate, and to put in writing the details of your negotiations.

Once you and the prospective buyer agree upon all the details of price and terms, you will complete the Purchase Agreement Checklist (see Figure 15.2). Use this checklist as a guideline in the preparation of documents for completion of sale. Either your **escrow agent*** or attorney can use this information; it can save them the time needed to ask questions.

QUALIFYING THE BUYER

Just because you have a prospect who has announced readiness to buy your home, this does not mean that you have a bona fide sale. Many a hopeful buyer may lack adequate income or the creditworthiness to attain financing, in which case it's futile to enter into a sales agreement.

If new financing is to be originated and the buyer has already arranged it, or a lender has already tentatively approved a mortgage loan in your price range, then it's not necessary to qualify the buyer beyond getting proof of these arrangements. In all other cases (loan assumption or a wrap-around loan), you must obtain certain information and qualify the buyer yourself. (For additional information on qualifying, see the section on qualification procedures in Chapter 3.)

SUMMARY

We can now compare the total cost of selling the property yourself to the cost of having it sold by a realtor who receives a 6 percent commission. Assuming a $80,000 selling price, the

---

*Escrow agent: Person responsible for carrying out the procedures necessary to transfer real property. In certain states a title company functions as an escrow company.

NOTE: This is not a legally binding agreement. It is simply a checklist to accommodate the drafting of a formal sales agreement between buyer and seller.

Name of prospective buyer(s) _____

_____

_____

currently residing at _____

_____phone _____

_____

are considering purchasing the property located at _____

_____

for a purchase price of $_____

Earnest money deposit of $_____ to be held in escrow

by _____

Buyer to assume existing loans of $ _____and $ _____

Or, buyer to originate new financing of $ _____

Real estate taxes last year were _____

Contingencies to be included in purchase agreement: _____

_____

_____

_____

Items *not included* in selling price: _____

_____

Items that *are included* in selling price: _____

_____

Seller will vacate the premises on _____

_____

Date of closing escrow _____

Seller to pay rent of $ _____per day if seller occupies premises after the close of escrow.

Legal description of property (use description given in title insurance or deed): _____

Figure 15.2 Purchase Agreement Checklist

realtor's commission would be $4800 ($80,000 × 6%). When you deduct your own costs of sale from this amount, the result is your savings.

The following are approximate costs you incur in selling the property yourself, not including normal closing costs which have to be paid regardless of whether you use a realtor:

For Sale signs	$ 60
Advertising	100
Copies of Property Information Sheet	5
Total cost	$165

Thus, you will make $4635 ($4800 − $165) or save that much, if you look at it that way, by selling the house yourself.

16 CHECKLIST OF IMPORTANT HIGHLIGHTS

In conclusion, here are some of the more important points raised in this book:

- Remember that real estate is essentially a long-term investment. If you hold on to your properties for an extended period, you'll gain the most from the following combination of benefits: appreciation, leverage, tax shelter, mortgage pay-off, and a higher return on cash invested than any other form of investment.

    Before 1986 tax reform, accelerated depreciation methods were allowed on income property. This meant that, for tax purposes, it was wise to sell income property every five to seven years because depreciation allowances were used up during this period. But this is no longer the case, because now only straight-line depreciation is allowed. This means that it takes at least 27.5 years to use up current depreciation allowances.

- Learn to specialize in investing in single-family homes. They offer the best opportunities, especially if you're a newcomer to realty investing. In particular, pay special attention to the Buy-Option strategy. It offers you profit potential far beyond other investment techniques. And don't forget the key ingredients to profitable opportunities (Chapter 4). They are: an undervalued fixer-upper, the proper financing, a large equity position, a motivated seller, the more land the better, and a good location in a thriving market. If your investment property has all these ingredients, you can rest assured that you've made a sound investment.

- With regard to financing, always try to assume low-interest-rate loans rather than originating new financing. If you have to originate new financing, stick with fixed-rate loans; remember, the only exception to this rule is for a short-term holding period—then, adjustable-rate financing can be advantageous if you hold the property four years or less.

- Remember the rules of hassle-free property management. Carefully screen your potential tenants so you can rent to people who will pay on time and care for your property. Don't forget to insert the no-hassle clause (tenant pays for repairs) into your rental agreement.

- With regard to tapping retirement income from equity in your home, remember that by selling on installment and renting a replacement home, you receive the biggest payoff and most reduced housing costs. If you plan on staying in your original home, the reverse mortgage offers more tax-free income than the other alternatives.

Building a retirement estate using your home as the foundation of a pyramid is very rewarding. If you're just getting started, be your own dream merchant. Envision yourself owning several rental properties, all appreciating in value year after year while giving you tax-free income. Your dreams will come true if you persevere and use the guidelines in this book.

Real estate: Just give it a part of yourself, and it will never fail you.

17 ANSWERS TO COMMONLY ASKED QUESTIONS ABOUT REAL ESTATE

Here are some selected questions and answers on loans and income taxes.

FIXED-RATE OR ARM?

Should I take out a mortgage now or wait until interest rates go lower? Which is better—the fixed-rate or adjustable-rate mortgage?

In response to your first question, there is no telling exactly when rates will go up or down. As a rule, however, interest rates are either in a rising or falling trend; seldom are they stable. Once the initial direction changes, rates will usually continue in that direction for a while until a new trend develops. Therefore, if interest rates are rising, it would be an educated guess that, if you waited, you'd pay more for a loan. On the other hand, if rates are falling, it would be likely that you could get a cheaper rate if you waited.

Regarding the question as to which is better—a fixed-rate mortgage or an ARM—it essentially depends on how long you plan to keep the mortgage. Both types of loans have inherent advantages and disadvantages.

As a rule, if you plan to own the property four years or less, the ARM will be more economical. If you own the property more than four years, the fixed-rate mortgage will cost you less. This is primarily due to lower initial rates on the ARM that in time gradually reach and surpass the rate of the fixed-rate mortgage.

Bear in mind that ARMs shift the risk of increasing interest rates from the lender to the borrower. In return, the borrower has certain caps that give protection against drastically increasing rates. More importantly, an ARM is assumable whereas most fixed-rate mortgages are not. This assumability is advantageous because the added flexibility makes your property more saleable.

DELINQUENT PAYMENTS

I noticed in my mortgage coupon that the due date of the payment is the first of the month; however, the lender doesn't charge a penalty unless the payment is made after the 15th of the month. Traditionally, I have paid the mortgage payment on the 10th and, as far as I can remember, I have not been assessed a late charge. Since my husband and I are planning to buy a new home, will our lender consider us late payers? And, if so, will it affect our ability to get a new loan?

No, don't worry about it. Your lender probably wished that he or she had more customers like you. If you study your mortgage agreement, you'll find that you have a grace period of 15 days during which the payment can be made without being considered delinquent. Certainly the lender would prefer to have your payment on the first, but getting it by the 15th isn't bad: Perhaps 10 percent of borrowers are chronically late and another 2 percent 30 days or more in arrears (when a loan is really considered to be delinquent). Only payments that were actually late will show up on the lender's record with a black mark. Since you always paid before the late-payment date, your loan record should be clean.

DEDUCTIBLE INTEREST

When is mortgage interest deductible?

Interest on your principal residence or a second home is 100 percent deductible. Mortgage interest deductibility isn't questionable unless you refinance your home or take out a second mortgage.

LIMITS ON INTEREST DEDUCTIONS

What are the limitations on the mortgage interest deduction?

Mortgage debt incurred on or after October 14, 1987 is divided into two kinds of indebtedness, each with a separate limit. The first is *acquisition indebtedness,* which is indebtedness used to acquire or substantially improve a residence. It was limited—in tax year 1988—to $1 million for up to two residences. The other kind is *home equity indebtedness,* which is any debt, other than acquisition indebtedness, that is secured by one or two residences. In tax year 1988, the deduction was limited to the fair market value of the residences plus improvements (not to exceed $100,000).

All mortgage interest incurred on or before October 13, 1987, regardless of amount or purpose, is "grandfathered," which in this case means it is treated as acquisition debt and is not subject to the $1 million limit.

INTEREST DEDUCTION FOR RAW LAND?

Can I deduct interest on a loan for land on which I plan to build a house?

Interest on unimproved land is considered personal interest, which eventually will be phased out as a deduction. In 1988, 40 percent of the interest was deductible; this percentage becomes 20 in 1989, 10 in 1990, and zero thereafter. Once you begin construction, 100 percent of mortgage interest is deductible.

POINTS

Are points deductible?

Yes, they are. Points on a loan to buy your house can be 100 percent deductible in the year the loan is issued. However, the points cannot be borrowed as part of the loan amount and have to be paid separately. If the points are added to the loan proceeds, they must be amortized over the life of the loan.

Points on a second mortgage or refinancing must be amortized over the term of the loan. When the house is sold, the remaining points are deductible. There is an exception: Points on VA or FHA loans are not deductible.

RV AS A SECOND HOME

I'm considering buying a recreational vehicle. Can I claim the motor home as a second home and deduct 100 percent of the interest from my taxes?

Yes—if you don't own another vacation home and the vehicle has a kitchen, bathroom, and bedroom. The deduction is also good for houseboats or for anything that the IRS considers a second vacation home. This is one of the few real estate deductions that were not eradicated by tax reform.

PRINCIPAL RESIDENCE

Does a recreational vehicle, mobile home, or boat qualify as a principal residence?

A principal residence is the place where you spend most of your time. A boat, mobile home, or RV qualifies as long as it has a kitchen, bathroom, and sleeping accommodations.

RENTAL DEDUCTIONS

I understand there are now limits on the deduction for payment of interest. I own four houses; two are rentals. Explain to me how interest deductions differ and what the limits are.

After 1988, the deduction for the payment of interest is limited to $1 million on your two nonrental homes. The cost of interest on the other rentals is an expense deducted from rental income. But this also has certain limits that depend on your adjusted gross income (AGI) and the date on which you bought the rentals. If your rental income minus rental expenses produces a net loss, you can deduct up to $25,000 from your salary income if your AGI is below $100,000. That deduction is reduced by 50 percent between $100,000 and $150,000 in AGI. Above $150,000, AGI losses are suspended; however, you can use them to offset future rental income.

There is one exception: If you purchased the rental property before October 23, 1986, you could deduct 40 percent of your disallowed losses in 1988 and 20 percent in 1989, whatever your income.

SELLING YOUR HOME

When I sell my home, do I have to pay taxes on the gain?

You can defer taxes on the gain as long as you buy, within two years, another home that's the same price or more than the home you sold. Additionally, if you are 55 or older, you have a once-in-a-lifetime, tax-free exemption on the first $125,000 in gain from the sale of your home. To qualify, you must have owned and lived in that home for at least three of the five years preceding its sale.

SELL HOME AND BUY LESS EXPENSIVE HOME

In the event I sell my house and buy a less expensive one, am I required to pay any taxes on the transaction?

Yes, you are required to pay taxes on the difference between the cost of the new residence and the adjusted sales price of your old house. The adjusted sales price of your old house equals the selling price less its cost basis and all costs incurred in selling it. The cost basis is determined by adding to the price of the home all the costs you incurred in buying it, plus the cost of improvements.

TIME-SHARE DEDUCTIONS

Besides my home, I own two time-share condominiums which I'm entitled to use one week of each year. How much interest is deductible on all three properties?

You can deduct 100 percent of the interest on the loans used to buy your principal residence and one of the time-shares (considered a second home). Interest paid on the other time-share is considered personal interest, which is gradually being phased out as a deduction. Personal interest was 40 percent deductible in 1988, 20 percent in 1989, 10 percent in 1990, and zero thereafter. The condo that the IRS considers your second home must meet certain requirements to be so considered. First, it must be used as security for the loan. Second, you actually have to own the property, even if for only one week of the year. Third, the way you take title to a time-share has a bearing: A "deeded" time-share qualifies; "right-to-use" agreement does not.

DEDUCTIBLE TAXES

What kind of taxes are deductible?

You can deduct state and local income taxes, personal property taxes, and real estate taxes. Sales taxes are not deductible.

LOSS OF MONEY ON SALE OF RESIDENCE

I sold my house for less than I paid for it. Is the loss deductible?

Unfortunately, no. If you sell your principal residence for less than you paid for it, consider it lost money; it's not tax deductible.

RENTAL UNIT TAX ADVANTAGES

My mother earns $32,000 annually and wants to buy a fourplex. If she lives in one unit and manages the others as rentals, what tax benefits would she receive?

Since your mother plans to reside in one of the units, she can deduct one-quarter of the mortgage interest and real estate taxes. On the remaining three-fourths, she can take a business deduction for interest and taxes. She can also depreciate the rental portion over 27.5 years and deduct the costs of maintenance and utilities. Because she plans to manage the building actively, she can deduct up to $25,000 in losses from the building from regular salary income, if the losses exceed any gains from other passive investments.

18 FORMS

The forms in this chapter are for you to use as you see fit. You may duplicate each form on a photocopier.

APPLICATION TO RENT

Investment in real estate is essentially a money-making enterprise, not a downtown charity mission. You have a lot invested, both in effort and money, so why in the world would you rent to a non-paying deadbeat or a malicious tenant? Yet, time after time, inexperienced property owners rent out their beloved properties without taking the time to properly qualify prospective tenants. Remember, you are essentially loaning your property to people for their use for a considerable period of time. A business relationship is about to develop, and if you rent to people who habitually pay late and aren't capable of taking reasonably good care of your property, you're in for plenty of trouble.

You can overcome most of the problems that novice landlords frequently encountered by properly qualifying your prospective renters. Good-paying tenants who will take good care of your property are a valuable asset. Here is some sound advice to assist you in judging whether or not your prospective tenants have good character and capability of meeting the terms of your rental agreement.

After your prospect has completely filled out the rental application (see Figure 18.1), review it carefully. Make sure everything is legible and complete. Make sure the name is correct, because later on if Jim Jones skips the premises, he will be easier to trace under his complete name of James Anthony

Jones. If more than one person will occupy the premises, get names of all the adults and find out who is responsible for rent payments.

Employment information is also very important. You definitely want to qualify the prospect on his or her ability to pay rent. As a general rule of thumb, a range of 28 percent to 33 percent of gross monthly income can safely be paid in rent. Lenders use a similar formula for making loans, wherein they allow 28 percent of gross income to be paid in mortgage payments. If the prospect has other debt obligations such as credit cards, car payments, and so on, then only a maximum of 28 percent could be applied toward rent; if not, then 33 percent of gross monthly income could be applied to rent payments.

If your prospect qualifies by his or her salary, then at a more appropriate time you should verify employment. A simple phone call to the employer is sufficient.

Credit References

This information, if it is necessary, will be supplied to a local credit bureau. After the prospect has completed the rental application, I usually ask to see his or her credit cards. If, in fact, he or she has active, up-to-date cards (which have not expired), this satisfies any doubts I may have about his or her creditworthiness. Just the fact that he or she has acquired major credit cards is usually a good indication of creditworthiness. One final credit check would be to call either his or her last or second-from-last landlord, and inquire into the prospect's character and rent-paying habits.

Spouse/Roommate (Part of Rental Application)

You gain added protection by having the spouse or roommate sign all the documents of the Rental Agreement. This way both parties are jointly responsible, and it may be easier to locate one of the tenants if the other skips.

Tenant Profile and Discrimination Laws

As a landlord you cannot, according to the law, refuse to rent to people because of their race, creed, color, national origin, sex, or marital status. This doesn't mean, however, that you are obligated to rent to anyone just because they have a fistful of money. In a multi-unit building, you should have certain standards that will promote harmony. For example, single adults prefer living in a building where other singles live. Likewise, families with children usually prefer to live in complexes which generally cater to families; senior citizens prefer to live where they're not annoyed by barking dogs and children at play. Therefore, set certain standards if you own multi-unit buildings and don't try to mix the elderly with the young, or singles with families.

INVENTORY OF FURNISHINGS

This form (Figure 18.2) should accompany the Rental Agreement for each unit. It essentially identifies items such as the refrigerator, stove, couch, etc., and denotes their current conditions. In the event of a lawsuit, the landlord can claim any damage, excluding reasonable wear and tear, against the security deposit. On the other hand, the tenants may counter that the damage was there prior to move-in. Except in cases of gross and negligent damage, a defense of "the damage was there before we moved in" is difficult to overcome unless proper documentation is provided.

At the time of move-in, have the tenants go through the unit, room by room, with you. Have the tenants fill out the Inventory of Furnishings, mark any comments, and return the form to you. If comments cannot be made in the space provided, have your tenants make any additional comments on the reverse side of the form; write "See reverse side."

TENANT RECORD CARD

This is a 5.5″ × 8″ card (Figure 18.3) used by the owner or manager. It is a record of all monies paid and due, plus other important tenant information.

Figure 18.1 Application to Rent

Name _____ Home Phone _____ Work Phone _____

Spouse/Roomate Name _____ Work Ph. _____

Unit to be occupied by _____ Adults and ____ Children and ____ Pets

Present Address _____ City _____ State ____ Zip ____

Current Landlord/Mgr's Name _____ Phone _____

Why are you leaving? _____

Previous Address _____ City _____ State ____ Zip ____

Landlord/Mgr's Name _____ Phone _____

Applicant's Birth Date _____ Soc. Sec. # _____ Driv. Lic. _____

Applicant's Employer_____ Position _____ How long _____

Applicant's Employer's Address _____ Gross monthly pay _____

Spouse/Roomate's Employer _____ Gross monthly pay _____

Credit References: Bank _____ Account # _____ Type _____

Other Active Reference _____ Account # _____

Spouse/Roomate Credit Ref. _____ Account # _____

In an emergency contact: _____ Phone _____

Address _____ City _____ State ____ Zip ____

List all motor vehicles, including RVs, to be kept at the dwelling unit. Include make, model, year, and license plate # for each.

Vehicle #1 _____. Vehicle #2 _____

License _____ License _____

Vehicle #3 _____

License _____

I (we) declare that the above information is correct and I (we) give my (our) permission for any reporting agency to release my credit file to undersigned landlord solely for the purposes of entering into a rental agreement. I (we) further authorize the Landlord or his agent to verify the above information including but not limited to contacting creditors, both listed herein or not, and present or former landlords.

Dated _____, 19 ____ Applicant _____

_____ Applicant _____

Landlord

Figure 18.2 Inventory of Furnishings

Rental unit address _____

Tenant _____ Inventory date _____, 19 _____

_____

Room	Item	Comments	Condition at Move-out

Tenant agrees that the above information is an accurate inventory and description and assumes responsibility for these items in the dwelling unit as of _____, 19 _____.

Move-in		Move-out	
_____ Date _____		_____ Date _____	
_____ Date _____		_____ Date _____	

NOTICE OF CHANGE IN RENTAL AGREEMENT (RENT RAISE)

This form (Figure 18.4) is used to change the rental rate. Usually, 30 days constitutes a suitable notice before increasing the rental rate. Original rental rates are found in the initial rental agreement. However, once the original term of the agreement expires, the landlord can, at his option, increase the rental rate.

KEY SIGNATURE _____

Address: _____

Orig. Move-In Date _____
Lease Dated _____ Exp. _____
Tenant Tel. No. _____

DEPOSIT

RENT

Date Due	Date Paid	Receipt Number	Paid To Noon	Amount Paid	Security Deposit	Cleaning Fee	Key Deposit #	Base Rent	Refrig-erator	Furniture	Parking	Month to Month	Additional Occupancy	Other Fireplace & Dishwasher	Air Conditioner	Utilities		Total Rent	Balance Due

Date
Due

BLDG. # _____ APT. _____ TYPE _____ FL. PL. _____ CLR. _____ NAME _____

Figure 18.3 Sample of Tenant Record Card

209

Figure 18.4 Notice of Change In Terms of Rental Agreement

Date _____

To _____, Tenant in possession of _____
_____.

[ ] Certified mail
[ ] Hand delivered
[ ] Regular mail

You are hereby notified that the terms of tenancy under which you occupy the above address are to be changed as follows:

Effective _____, 19 ____, your rent will be increased by $ _____ per month for a total of $ _____ each month.

_____
Landlord/Agent

REMINDERS TO PAY RENT

Delinquency by your tenants should not be tolerated. Good landlords should react predictably and immediately to nonpayment of rent when it is due. Slow-paying tenants will usually react to this predictability and make the rent a high priority on their list of payments. Normally there is a three-day grace period after the rent due date. If the rent is not received within three days of due date, action has to be taken. Collection experts agree that a first notice be sent within five days of the due date and a second notice after seven days. In the event your slow-paying tenant has a history of delinquency, a Three-Day Notice to Pay or Quit the Premises (Figure 18.5) could be used in place of the second notice.

RENTAL AGREEMENT

I have supplied you with a sample residential lease (Figure 18.6). You can either use it or buy a residential lease form at a stationery store. The following are important points to consider, taken from the sample rental agreement and retaining their paragraph number for reference:

3. Terms: Your rental agreement can either be month-to-month or a year.

4. Rent: The amount of rent to be paid must be spelled out. Be sure to include a late fee, which is commonly five percent of the monthly rent.

9. Repairs and Maintenance: The clause "except for the first $100 in cost which the Tenant pays" is called the "no-hassle

---

To _____   Date _____

   Just a reminder that your rent was due on _____. According to the terms of your Rental Agreement, rent more than _____days past due requires a late charge of $ _____. We would appreciate your prompt payment.

                                        Thank you,

                                        _____
                                        Landlord/Agent

To _____   Date _____

   Your rent is now past due. Due date _____. As of this reminder, the past-due rent and late charges total $ _____.
   You must settle this account or our legal options will have to be considered. Therefore, please act to remedy this matter immediately.

                                        Thank you,

                                        _____
                                        Landlord/Agent

**Figure 18.5 Three-Day Reminder to Pay Rent and
Five-Day Reminder to Pay Rent**

Figure 18.6 Rental Agreement (Residential Lease)

1. This Lease made this _____ day of _____, 19 _____, by and between _____,
hereinafter called Landlord, and _____,
hereinafter called Tenant.

2. *Description*: Witnesseth, the Landlord, in consideration of the rents to be paid and the covenants and agreements to be performed by the Tenant, does hereby lease unto the Tenant the following described premises located thereon situated in the City of _____, County of _____,
State of _____, commonly known as _____
_____.

3. *Terms*: For the term of _____ (months/years) commencing on _____, 19 _____, and ending on _____
_____, 19 _____.

4. *Rent*: Tenant shall pay Landlord, as rent for said premises, the sum of _____ dollars ($ _____) per month payable in advance on the first day of each month during the term hereof at Landlord's address above or said other place as Landlord may hereafter designate in writing. Tenant agrees to pay a $25 late fee if rent is not paid within five days of due date.

5. *Security Deposit*: Landlord herewith acknowledges the receipt of _____ _____ dollars ($ _____), which he is to retain as security for the faithful performance of the provisions of this Lease. If Tenant fails to pay rent, or defaults with respect to any provision of this Lease, Landlord may use the security deposit to cure the default or compensate Landlord for all damages sustained by Landlord. Tenant shall immediately on demand reimburse Landlord the sum equal to that portion of security deposit expended by Landlord so as to maintain the security deposit in the sum initially deposited with Landlord. If Tenant performs all obligations under this Lease, the security deposit, or that portion thereof that was not previously applied by Landlord, shall be returned to Tenant within 21 days after the expiration of this Lease, or after Tenant has vacated the premises.

6. *Possession*: It is understood that if the Tenant shall be unable to enter into and occupy the premises hereby leased at the time above provided, by reason of the said premises not being ready for occupancy, or by reason of holding over of any previous occupancy of said premises, the Landlord shall not be liable in damage to the Tenant therefore, but during the period the Tenant shall be unable to occupy said premises as hereinbefore provided, the rental therefore shall be abated and the Landlord is to be the sole judge as to when the premises are ready for occupancy.

7. *Use*: Tenant agrees that said premises during the term of this Lease shall be used and occupied by _____ adults and _____ children, and _____ animals, and for no purpose whatsoever other than a residence, without the written consent of the Landlord, and that Tenant will not use the premises for any

purpose in violation of any law, municipal ordinance, or regulation, and at any breach of this agreement the Landlord may at his option terminate this Lease and re-enter and repossess the leased premises.

8. *Utilities*: Tenant will pay for all charges for all water supplied to the premises and pay for all gas, heat, electricity, and other services supplied to the premises, except as herein provided: _____.

9. *Repairs and Maintenance*: The Landlord shall at his expense, except for the first $100 in cost which the Tenant pays, keep and maintain the exterior walls, roof, electrical wiring, heating and air-conditioning system, water heater, built-in appliances, and water lines in good condition and repair, except where damage has been caused by negligence or abuse of the Tenant, in which case Tenant shall repair same at his sole expense.

Tenant hereby agrees that the premises are now in good condition and shall at his sole expense maintain the premises and appurtenances in the manner in which they were received, reasonable wear and tear excepted.

The _____ agrees to maintian landscaping and swimming pool (if any). Tenant agrees to adequately water landscaping.

10. *Alterations and Additions*: The Tenant shall not make any alterations, additions, or improvements to said premises without the Landlord's written consent. All alterations, additions, or improvements made by either of the parties hereto upon the premises, except movable furniture, shall be the property of the Landlord and shall remain upon and be surrendered with the premises at the termination of this Lease.

11. *Assignment*: The Tenant will not assign or transfer this lease or sublet said premises without the written consent of the Landlord.

12. *Default*: If the Tenant shall abandon or vacate said premises before the end of the term of this lease, or if default shall be made by the tenant in the payment of said rent or any part hereof, or if the Tenant shall fail to perform any of the Tenant's agreements in this lease, then and in each and every instance of such abandonment or default, the Tenant's right to enter said premises shall be suspended, and the Landlord may at his option enter said premises and remove and exclude the Tenant from said premises.

13. *Entry by Landlord*: Tenant shall allow the Landlord or his agents to enter the premises at all reasonable times and upon reasonable notice for the purpose of inspecting or maintaining the premises or to show it to prospective tenants or purchasers.

14. *Attorney's fees*: The Tenant agrees to pay all costs, expenses, and reasonable attorney's fees including obtaining advice of counsel incurred by Landlord in enforcing by legal action or otherwise any of Landlord's rights under this lease or under any law of this state.

15. *Holding Over*: If Tenant, with the Landlord's consent, remains in possession of the premises after expiration of the term of this lease, such possession will be deemed a month-to-month tenancy at a rental equal to the last monthly

Figure 18.6 (continued)

rental, and upon all the provisions of this lease applicable to such a month-to-month tenancy.

The parties hereto have executed this Lease on the date first above written.

<table>
<tr><td>**Landlord**</td><td></td><td>**Tenant**</td></tr>
<tr><td>By: _____</td><td></td><td>By: _____</td></tr>
<tr><td></td><td></td><td>By: _____</td></tr>
</table>

Figure 18.6 (continued)

clause." If you buy a rental agreement form at a stationery store, be sure to insert this clause into it. And be sure to inform your tenants verbally that the first $100 in repair is their responsibility. This way you can avoid many late-night phone calls from tenants who need minor repair work done.

GLOSSARY OF REAL ESTATE DEFINITIONS

Abandonment The voluntary relinquishment of rights of ownership or another form of interest (an easement) by failure to use the property over an extended period of time.

Absentee landlord A lessor of real property (usually the owner) who does not reside on any portion of the property.

Abstract of title A summary of the conveyances, transfers, and any other data relied on as evidence of title, together with any other elements of record which may impair the title. Still in use in some states, but giving way to the use of title insurance.

Accelerated depreciation Depreciation occurring at a rate faster than the normal rate. This form of depreciation is usually used for special assets for income tax purposes.

Acceleration clause A clause in a mortgage or trust deed giving the lender the right to call all monies owed to be immediately due and payable upon the happening of a certain stated event.

Acceptance A legal term denoting acceptance of an offer. A buyer offers to buy and the seller accepts the offer.

Access right A right to enter and exit one's property.

Accretion Gradual deposit of soil from a waterway onto the adjoining land. The additional land generally becomes the property of the owner of the shore or bank, except where local statutes specify otherwise.

Accrued depreciation The amount of depreciation accumulated over a period of time in the accounting system for replacement of an asset.

Acknowledgment A formal declaration of execution of a document before an authorized official (usually a notary public) by a person who has executed (signed) a document.

Acre   A measure of land, equal to 160 sq. rods (43,560 sq. ft.). An acre is approximately 209 × 209 feet.

Addendum   Something added. A list or other items added to a document, letter, contract, escrow instructions, etc.

Adjustable-rate mortgage (ARM)   Mortgage with an interest rate that can change as often as specified.

Adjusted-cost basis   The value of an asset on the accounting books of a taxpayer that is the original cost plus improvements less depreciation.

Adjusted sales price   Equals, for income tax purposes, the selling price of your house less its acquisition cost and all the costs incurred in selling it.

Adverse land use   A use of land that causes the surrounding property to lose value, such as a truck terminal adjacent to a residential area.

Adverse possession   A method of acquiring title by open and notorious possession under an evident claim or right. Specific requirements for time of possession vary state to state.

Affidavit   A written statement or declaration sworn to or affirmed before an official who has the authority to administer affirmation. An oath.

Agency agreement (listing)   A listing agreement between the seller of real property and a broker wherein the broker's commission is protected against a sale by other agents but not by the principal (seller). Often called a nonexclusive agency listing.

Agent   A person authorized to represent or act for another in business matters.

Agreement of sale   A written contract between buyer and seller, in which both parties are in full agreement on the terms and conditions of the sale.

Alienation   The transfer of property from one person to another.

Alienation clause   A clause within a loan instrument calling for a debt to be paid in its entirety upon the transfer of ownership of the secured property. Similar to a "due-on-sale" clause.

All-Inclusive Trust Deed (AITD)   Same as wrap-around mortgage except a deed of trust is the security instrument instead of a mortgage.

Alluvion   Soil deposited by accretion.

Amenities   Attractive or desirable features of a property, such as a swimming pool or ocean view.

American Land Title Association (ALTA)   A group of title insurance companies that issues title insurance to lenders.

Amortization   The liquidation of a financial obligation using regular equal payments on an installment basis.

Annuity   (1) Cash payment over a given period. (2) A fixed amount given or left by will, paid periodically.

Appraisal   An estimate and opinion of value: an objective conclusion resulting from an analysis of pertinent data.

Appreciation   Increase in value of property from improvements or the elimination of negative factors.

Appurtenance   Something belonging to the land and conveyed with it, such as buildings, fixtures, and rights.

ARM   See adjustable-rate mortgage.

ASHI   American Society of Home Inspectors.

Assemblage   Process of acquiring contiguous properties into one overall parcel for a specific use or to increase value of the whole.

Assessed value   Value placed on property by the tax assessor.

Assessment   The valuation of property for the purpose of levying a tax, or the amount of the tax levied.

Assessor   One appointed to assess property for taxation.

Assigned mortgage   A note which is transferred to another party. See also *assignment*.

Assignee   One who receives an assignment. (Assignor: one who owns property assigned.)

Assignment   A transfer or making over to another the whole of any property, real or personal, or of any estate or right therein. To assign is to transfer.

Assumption of mortgage   The agreement of a buyer to assume the liability of an existing mortgage. Normally, the lender has to approve the new borrower before the existing borrower is released from the liability.

Attachment   Seizure of property by court order, usually done in a pending lawsuit to make property available in case of judgment.

Balance sheet   A financial statement that shows the true condition of a business or individual as of a particular date. Discloses assets, liabilities, and net worth.

Balloon payment   The final installment paid at the end of the term of a note: used only when preceding installments were not sufficient to pay off the note in full.

Bankruptcy   Procedure of federal law to seize the property of a debtor and divide the proceeds among the creditors.

Base and meridian   Imaginary lines used by surveyors to find and describe the location of public or private lands.

Benchmark A mark, used by surveyors, that is permanently fixed in the ground to denote height of that point in relation to sea level.

Beneficiary The lender involved in a note and trust deed; one entitled to the benefit of a trust.

Bequeath To give or leave property by a will.

Bill of sale An instrument used to transfer personal property.

Blank mortgage (trust deed) A single mortgage, or trust deed, that covers more than one piece of real estate.

Blighted area A declining area where property values are affected by destructive economic or natural forces.

Block busting A method of informing a community of the fact that people of a different race or religion are moving into the neighborhood: this often causes property values to drop, thereby enabling homes to be obtained at below market value.

Boardfoot A unit of measuring lumber. One boardfoot is 12 by 12 by 1 inch, or 144 cubic inches.

Bond An insurance agreement by which one party is insured against loss or default by another. In the construction business a performance bond ensures the interested party that the contractor will complete the project. A bond can also be a method of financing debt by a government or corporation; the bond is interest-bearing and has priority over stock in terms of security.

Book value The value of an asset plus improvements less depreciation.

Boot A term used when trading property. "Boot" is the additional value given when trading properties in order to equalize values.

Bottom land Low-lying ground such as a valley; also, low land along a waterway formed by alluvial deposits.

Breach Violation of an obligation in a contract.

British Thermal Unit (BTU) Describes the capacity of heating and cooling systems. It is the unit of heat required to raise one pound of water one degree Fahrenheit.

Broker (real estate) An agent licensed by the state to carry on the business of dealing in real estate. He or she usually receives a commission for services of bringing together buyers and sellers, or tenants and landlords.

Building code A set of laws that control the design, materials, and similar factors in the construction of buildings.

Building line A line set by law or deed marking a certain distance from the street line, in front of which an owner cannot build a lot. Also known as a setback line.

Built-ins Items that are part of the structure and not movable, such as stoves, ovens, cabinets, and built-in dishwashers.

Built-up roof A form of level roof consisting of layers of roofing materials covered with fine gravel.

Business opportunity The sale or lease of a business and good will of an existing business enterprise.

Buyers' market A market condition in which more homes are for sale than there are interested buyers.

Buy-Option: See *Lease with option to purchase.*

Capital expenditures Money spent by a business on improvements such as land, building, and machinery.

Capital gains A term used for income tax purposes; it represents the gain realized from the sale of an asset less the purchase price and deductible expenses. (Before the 1986 tax reform, capital gains rules allowed 60 percent exclusion from taxes on the sale of an asset if it was a capital gain.)

Capitalization An appraising term used in determining value by considering net-operating income and a percentage of reasonable return on investment.

Capitalization rate A percentage used by an investor to determine the value of income property through capitalization.

Cash flow The owner's spendable income after operating expenses and debt service are deducted.

Caveat emptor A legal phrase meaning "let the buyer beware." The buyer takes the risk when purchasing an item without the protection of warranties.

Certificate of Reasonable Value (CRV) An appraisal of real property issued by the Veteran's Administration.

Chain of title A history of conveyances and encumbrances affecting the title to real property as far back as records are available.

Chattel Personal property.

Chattel mortgage A mortgage on personal property, as distinguished from one on real property.

Client One who employs the services of an attorney, real estate agent, insurance agent, etc.

Closing In the sale of real estate, the final moment when all documents are executed and recorded and the sale is complete. Also a general selling term where a salesperson is attempting to sell something and the buyer agrees to purchase.

Closing costs   Incidental expenses incurred with the sale of real property, such as appraisal fees, title insurance, termite report, and so on.

Closing statement   A list of the final accounting of all monies of both buyer and seller, prepared by an escrow agent. It notes all costs each must pay at the completion of a real estate transaction.

Cloud on title   An encumbrance on real property that affects the rights of the owner and which often keeps the title from being marketable until the "cloud" is removed.

Collateral security   A separate obligation attached to another contract pledging something of value to guarantee performance of the contract.

Commercial bank   An institution for checking accounts, loans, savings accounts, and other services usually not found in savings and loan associations. Banks are active in installment loans on vehicles and boats and construction financing rather than on long-term real estate financing. See also Institutional Lenders.

Common area   That area owned in common by owners of condominiums and planned unit-development homes within a subdivision.

Compound interest   Interest paid on the original principal and on interest accrued.

Condemnation   A declaration by governing powers that a structure is unfit for use.

Conditional sales contract   A contract for the sale of property where the buyer has possession and use, but the seller retains title until the conditions of the contract have been fulfilled. Also known as a Land Contract.

Condominium   A system of individual ownership of units in a multi-unit structure where each space is individually owned but each owner jointly owns the common areas and land.

Conformity, principle of   An appraising term stating that uniformity throughout a certain area produces highest value.

Conservator   A court-appointed guardian.

Consideration   Anything of value given to induce someone into entering into a contract.

Construction loan   The short-term financing of improvements on real estate. Once the improvements are completed, a "take-out" loan for a longer term is used to pay off the existing construction loan.

Contingency   A condition upon which a valid contract is dependent. For example, the sale of a house is contingent upon the buyer's obtaining adequate financing.

Contract   An agreement between two or more parties, written or oral, to do or no to do certain things.

Contract of sale   Same as Conditional Sales Contract or a Land Contract.

Conventional loan   A loan, usually on real estate, that is not backed by the federal agencies of FHA and VA.

Convertible ARM   Adjustable-rate mortgage which can convert to a fixed-rate mortgage.

Conveyance   The transfer of title to land from one party to another.

Cooperative apartment   A building with two or more units in which the unit owners are required to purchase stock in the corporation that owns the property. The co-op was a forerunner to the condominium and is not as popular because of the difficulty in financing, since there is no individual ownership of each unit.

Corporation   A legal entity having certain powers and duties of a natural person, together with rights and liabilities of both, distinct and apart from those persons composing it.

Cost approach   A method of appraisal whereby the estimated cost of a structure is calculated, less the land value and depreciation.

Counteroffer   An offer in response to an offer. A offers to buy B's house for $80,000 although it is listed for $85,000. B counteroffers A by stating that he/she will sell the house to A for $81,000. The $81,000 is a counteroffer.

Covenants   Agreements written into deeds and other instruments stating performance or nonperformance of certain acts or noting certain uses or nonuses of the property.

CPM   Certified Property Manager.

Cul de sac   A dead-end street with a turn-around included.

Current assets   An accounting term denoting assets that can readily be converted into cash, such as short-term accounts receivable and common stocks.

Current liabilities   Short-term debts.

D.B.A. (Doing Business As)   A business name or identification.

Dedication   The donation by an owner of private property for public use.

Deed   A written instrument that when executed conveys title of real property.

Default   Failure to fulfill or discharge an obligation or to perform any act that has been agreed to in writing.

Defendant   The individual or entity against whom a civil or criminal action is brought.

Deferred payments   Payments to begin in the future.

Deflation   Opposite of inflation. The price of goods and services decrease in relation to the money available to buy them.

Delivery   The placing of property in the possession of the grantee.

Demise   A transfer of an estate by lease or will.

Demographics   Statistics. Data used by certain businesses (especially chain stores) such as the traffic count regarding a possible new location.

Density   The amount of crowding together of buildings, people, or other given things.

Depletion   The reduction or loss in value of an asset.

Deposit receipt   The form used to accept the earnest-money deposit to secure the offer for the purchase of real property.

Depreciation   Loss of value of an asset brought about by age (positive deterioration) or functional and economic obsolescence. Percentage reduction of property value year by year for tax purposes.

Depression   That part of a business cycle where unemployment is high and production and overall purchasing by the public is low. A severe recession.

Deterioration   The gradual wearing away of a building from exposure to the elements. Also referred to as physical depreciation.

Devise   A gift of real estate by will.

Diluvium   A deposit of land left by a flood.

Diminishing returns   An economic theory stating that an increase in capital or manpower will not increase production proportionately (four laborers may do less than four times the work of one laborer; two laborers may do more than twice the work of one laborer). The return diminishes when production is proportionately less than input.

Directional growth   The path of development of an urban area. Used to determine where future development will be most profitable.

Divided interest   Different interest in the same property, as in interest of the owner, lessee, or mortgagee.

Documentary tax stamps   Stamps affixed to a deed denoting the amount of transfer tax paid.

Domicile   The place where a person has a permanent home.

Double-declining depreciation   An accelerated method of depreciating an asset in which double the amount of straight-line depreciation is used.

Dower   The portion of her husband's estate that a wife inherits on his death.

Down payment   Cash or other consideration paid toward a purchase by the buyer, as opposed to that amount which is financed.

Due-on-sale clause   A condition written into a financial instrument which gives the lender the right to require immediate repayment of the unpaid balance if the property is sold without consent of the lender.

Easement   The legal right-of-way that permits an owner to cross another's land so as to get to his or her own property. Easement is appurtenant to the land and thus cannot be sold off separately and must be transferred with the title to the land of which it is part. Other forms of rights and privileges with respect to adjacent or nearby land can be created by agreement and are also called easements to the property.

Economic life   The period over which property will yield a return on the investment.

Economic obsolescence   Loss of useful life and desirability of a property through economic forces, such as change in zoning, changes in traffic flow, and so on, rather than deterioration.

Economic rent   The current market rental based on comparable rent for a similar unit.

Effective age   The age of a structure estimated by its condition as opposed to its actual age.

Egress   The right to go out across the land of another.

Elevation   The height above sea level. Architecturally, the view looking at the front of a structure.

Emblements   Crops growing on the land.

Eminent domain   The right of the government to acquire private property for public use by condemnation. The owner must be fully compensated.

Encroachment   Trespass. The building or any improvements partly or wholly on the property of another.

Encumbrance   Anything that affects or limits the fee simple title to property, such as mortgages, trust deeds, easements, or restrictions of any kind. Liens are special encumbrances that make the property security for the debt.

Entity   An existence or being, as in a corporation or business, rather than an individual person.

Entrepreneur   An independent businessperson taking risks for profit, as opposed to a salaried employee working for someone else.

Equity   The value that an owner has in property over and above the liens against it. A legal term based on fairness rather than strict interpretation of the law.

Equity build-up   The reduction in the difference between property value and the amount of the lien as regular payments are made. The equity increases (builds up) on an amortized loan as the proportion of interest payment gets smaller, causing the amount going toward principal to increase.

Equity participation   See equity sharing.

Equity partnership   See equity sharing.

Equity sharing   Shared ownership of real property. Also known as shared equity, equity participation, equity partnership, and shared appreciation.

Escalation clause   A clause in a lease providing for an increase in rent at a future time because of increased costs to lessor, as in cost-of-living index, tax increases, and so on.

Escheat   The reverting of property to the state in the absence of heirs.

Escrow   A neutral third party who carries out the provisions of an agreement between two or more parties.

Estate   The ownership interest of a person in real property. Often used to describe a large home with spacious grounds. Also a deceased person's property.

Estate for years   Any estate for a specific period of time. A lease.

Exclusive right-to-sell listing   A written contract between agent and owner in which the agent has the right to collect a commission if the listed property is sold by anyone during the terms of agreement.

Executor   The person appointed in a will to carry out the terms of the will.

Face value   The value stated on the face of notes, mortgages, and so on, without consideration of any discounting.

Fair market value   The price a property will bring given that both buyer and seller are fully aware of market conditions and comparable properties.

Feasibility survey   A study of an area prior to development of a project in order to determine whether the project will be successful.

Fed   See Federal System Reserve System.

Federal Deposit Insurance Corporation (FDIC)   The federal corporation that insures bank depositors against loss up to a specified amount, currently $100,000.

Federal Home Loan Bank Board The board that charters and regulates Federal Savings and Loan Associations and Federal Home Loan Banks.

Federal Home Loan Banks Regulated by the Federal Home Loan Bank Board. Currently 11 regional branches where banks, savings and loans, insurance companies, or similar institutions may join the system and borrow for the purpose of making available home-financing money. Its purpose is to make a permanent supply of financing available for home loans.

Federal Home Loan Mortgage Corporation (FHLMC) (Freddie Mac) A federal agency that purchases first mortgages from members of the Federal Reserve System and the Federal Home Loan Bank system.

Federal Housing Administration (FHA) The federal agency that insures first mortgages on homes (and other projects), enabling lenders to extend more lenient terms to borrowers.

Federal National Mortgage Association (FNMA) (Fannie Mae) A private corporation that purchases first mortgages at discounts.

Federal Reserve System Commonly referred to as the "Fed," it consists of a twelve-member Federal Open Market Committee, twelve Fed branches, plus approximately 6,000 member banks. Its primary purpose is to control the supply of money.

Federal Savings and Loan Insurance Corporation (FSLIC) A federal corporation that insures deposits in savings and loan associations up to a specified amount, currently $125,000.

Fee simple Ownership of title to property without any limitation, which can be sold, left by will, or inherited.

Fiduciary A person in a position of trust and confidence, as between principal and broker; broker as fiduciary owes loyalty to the principal, which cannot be breached under rules of agency.

First mortgage A mortgage having priority over all other voluntary liens against a specific property.

Fixed-rate mortgage A mortgage loan wherein the rate of interest charged the borrower remains constant over its term.

Fixtures Items, such as plumbing, electrical fixtures, etc., affixed to buildings or land usually in such a way that they cannot be removed without damage to themselves or the property.

Foreclosure Procedure in which property pledged for security for a debt is sold at public auction to pay the debt in the event of default in payment and terms.

Free and clear A specific property has no liens, especially voluntary liens, against it.

Front footage The linear measurement along the front of a parcel. That portion of the parcel that fronts the street or walkway.

Functional obsolescence Loss in value of out-of-date or poorly designed equipment while newer equipment and structures have been invented since its construction.

Government National Mortgage Association (GNMA) (Ginnie Mae) Purchases first mortgages at discounts, similar to that of FNMA.

Graduated lease A lease that provides for rental adjustments, often based upon future determination of the cost-of-living index. Used for the most part in long-term leases.

Graduated payment mortgage (GPM) Increases in payment over its term.

Grant A transfer of interest in real property, such as an easement.

Grantee One to whom the grant is made.

Grantor The one who grants the property or its rights.

Gross income Total scheduled income from property before any expenses are deducted.

Gross-income multiplier A general appraising rule of thumb that when multiplied by the gross annual income of a property will estimate the market value. For example, the property sells for 7.2 times the gross.

Gross lease A lease obligating the lessor to pay all or part of the expenses incurred on a leased property.

Ground lease A lease of vacant land.

Ground rent Rend paid for vacant land.

Growing equity mortgage (GEM) Increases in payment over a specified term. Increases are applied directly to principal reduction.

Hardwood Wood, such as oak, maple, and walnut, used for interior finish, as opposed to certain other soft woods.

Highest and best use An appraisal term for the use of land that will bring the highest economic return over a given time.

Homeowners association An association of homeowners within a community formed to improve and maintain the quality of the community. An association formed by the developer of condominiums or planned-unit-developments.

Homestead A declaration by the owner of a home that protects the home against judgments up to specified amounts provided by certain state laws.

Hypothecate To give a thing as security without giving up possession of it, as with mortgaging real property.

Impound account   A trust account held for the purpose of paying taxes, insurance, and other periodic expenses incurred with real property.

Improvements   A general term to describe buildings, roads, and utilities that have been added to raw (unimproved) land.

Inflation   The increase in an economy over its true or natural growth. Usually identified with rapidly increasing prices.

Installment note   A note that provides for regular monthly payments to be paid on the date specified in the instrument.

Institutional lenders   Banks, savings and loans, or other businesses who make loans to the public during their ordinary course of business, as opposed to individuals who fund loans.

Instrument   A written legal document.

Intangible value   The good will or well-advertised name of an established business.

Interest   (1) money charged for the use of money (principal). (2) a share or right in some property.

Interim loan   A short-term loan usually for real estate improvements during the period of construction.

Intestate   A person who dies without having made a will.

Intrinsic value   The value of a thing by itself without certain aspects which will add value to some and not to others, as with a vintage Rolls Royce, which might have value to a car collector, but to few others.

Investment   The laying out of money in the purchase of some form of property intending to earn a profit.

Involuntary lien   A lien that attaches to property without consent of the owner, such as tax liens as opposed to voluntary liens (mortgages).

Joint tenancy   Joint ownership by two or more persons with right of survivorship. Upon the death of a joint tenant, the interest does not go to the heirs but to the remaining joint tenants.

Junior mortgage   A mortgage lower in priority than a first mortgage, such as second and third mortgages.

Land contract   A contract for the sale of property where the buyer has possession and use, but the seller retains title until certain conditions of the contract have been fulfilled. Same as a conditional sales contract.

Land grant   A gift of public land by the federal government.

Landlord   The owner of rented property.

Lease   A contract between the owner of real property, called the lessor, and another person or party referred to as the lessee, covering the conditions by which the lessee may occupy and use the property.

Lease with option to purchase   A lease under which the lessee has the option to purchase the leased property, the terms of which must be set forth in the lease.

Legacy   A gift of personal property by will.

Legal description   The geographical identification of a parcel of land.

Legatee   One who receives personal property from a will.

Lessee   One who contracts to rent property under a lease.

Lessor   An owner who contracts into a lease with a tenant (lessee).

Leverage   The use of a small amount of cash to control a much greater value of assets.

Liability   A term covering all types of debts and obligations.

Lien   An encumbrance against real property for money as in taxes, mortgages, and judgments.

Life estate   An estate in real property for the life of a person.

Limited partnership   A partnership of one or more general partners that operates a business along with one or more limited partners who contribute capital. This arrangement limits certain of the partners' liability to the amount of money contributed.

Liquidate   Disposal of property or assets or the settlement of debts.

Lis pendens   A recorded legal notice showing pending litigation of real property. Anyone acquiring an interest in such property after the recording of *lis pendens* could be bound by the outcome of the litigation.

Listing   A contract between owner and broker to sell the owner's real property.

Loan to value ratio (LTVR)   The ratio, expressed as a percentage, of the amount of a loan to the value of real property.

Long-term capital gain   Prior to the 1986 tax reform it was a preferential tax treatment excluding 60 percent of the gain incurred on the sale of an asset held for at least six months.

MAI (Member Appraisal Institute)   A designation issued to a member of the American Institute of Real Estate Appraisers after meeting specific qualifications.

Maintenance reserve   Money held in reserve to cover anticipated maintenance expenses.

Margin   For lending purposes, that amount added to a certain index rate which results in the interest rate charged the borrower.

Marketable title   A saleable title free of objectionable liens or encumbrances.

Market-data approach   An appraisal method to determine value by comparing similar properties to the subject property.

Market value   The price a buyer will pay and a seller will accept, both being fully informed of market conditions.

Master plan   A comprehensive zoning plan to allow a city to grow in an orderly manner.

Mechanics lien   A lien on a specific property for labor or materials that have contributed to an improvement on that property.

Metes and bounds   A legal description used in describing the property through descriptions of boundary lines.

Mineral rights   Ownership of the minerals beneath the ground. The owner of mineral rights doesn't necessarily own the surface land.

Moratorium   Temporary suspension of the enforcement of liability for a debt.

Mortgage   An instrument by which property is hypothecated to secure the payment of a debt.

Mortgage broker   A person who, for a fee, brings together the lender with the borrower. Also known as a loan broker.

Mortgage Guaranty Insurance Corporation (MGIC)   Private corporation that insures mortgage loans.

Mortgagee   One who lends the money and receives the mortgage.

Mortgagor   One who borrows on a property and gives a mortgage as security.

Multiple listing service (MLS)   A listing taken by a member of an organization of brokers, whereby all members have an opportunity to find a buyer.

Net income   Gross income less operating expenses.

Net lease   A lease requiring tenant to pay all or part of the expenses on leased property in addition to the stipulated rent.

Net listing   A listing whereby an agent may retain as compensation all sums received over and above a net price to the owner. Illegal in some states.

Net worth   Total assets less liabilities of an individual, corporation, or business.

Nonexclusive listing A listing in which the agent has an exclusive listing with respect to other agents; however, the owner may sell the property without being liable for a commission.

Notary public One who is authorized by federal or state government to attest authentic signatures and administer oaths.

Note A written instrument acknowledging a debt and promising payment.

Notice to quit A notice issued by landlord to tenant to vacate rented property, usually for nonpayment of rent or breach of contract.

Offer A presentation to form a contract or agreement.

Open listing An authorization given by an owner to a real estate agent to sell the owner's property. Open listings may be given to more than one agent without liability, and only the one who secures a buyer on satisfactory terms gets paid a commission.

Operating expenses Expenses relevant to income-producing property, such as taxes, management, utilities, insurance, and other day-to-day costs.

Option A right given, for consideration, to purchase or lease property upon stipulated terms within a specific period of time.

Passive activity New definition under the 1986 tax reform. A passive activity is any activity that involves the conduct of trade or business in which you do not materially participate. Any rental activity will be a passive activity even if you do materially participate. Prior to the tax reform, passive losses could offset other forms of income; subsequent to the act, the taxpayer is limited to the amount of losses that can offset other income.

Percentage lease A lease on property in which normally a minimum specified rent is paid or a percentage of gross receipts of the lessee is paid, whichever is higher.

Personal property Property that is not real property (i.e., not real estate).

Planned unit development Five or more individually owned lots where one or more other parcels are owned in common or there are reciprocal rights in one or more other parcels; subdivision.

Plat book A book containing plat maps of a certain area.

Plat map A map or plan of a specified parcel of land.

Point One percent. A 1-point fee often charged by the lender to originate the loan. On FHA and VA loans, the seller pays points to accommodate the loan.

Power of attorney An instrument authorizing a person to act as the agent of the person granting the power.

Preliminary title report   The report of condition of the title before a sale or loan transaction. Once completed, a title insurance policy is issued.

Prepayment penalty   A penalty within a note, mortgage, or trust deed, imposing a penalty if the debt is paid in full before the end of it's term.

Prime lending rate   The most favorable interest rate charged by an institutional lender to its best customers.

Principal   The employer of an agent. Also, the amount of debt, not including interest.

Private Mortgage Insurance (PMI)   Insurance on a portion of the first mortgage allowing the lender to offer more lenient terms to a borrower.

Proration of taxes   To divide or prorate the taxes equally or proportionately to time of use.

Purchase agreement   An agreement between buyer and seller denoting price and terms of the sale.

Purchase money mortgage   A mortgage given by the buyer to the seller as part of the purchase consideration.

Pyramid   To build an estate by multiple acquisitions of properties using the initial properties as a base for further investment.

Quitclaim deed   A deed used to remove clouds on a title by relinquishing any right, title, or interest that the grantor may have.

Real Estate Investment Trust (REIT)   A method of group investment with certain tax advantages. It is governed by federal and state laws.

Realtor   A real estate broker holding membership in a real estate board affiliated with the National Association of Realtors.

Redemption   The buying back of one's property after it has been lost through foreclosure. Payment of delinquent taxes after sale to the state.

Rent   Consideration, usually money, for the occupancy and use of real property.

Replacement-cost method   A method of appraisal to determine value by determining an exact replica.

Request for notice of default   A request by a lender that is recorded for notification in the case of default by a loan with priority.

Reverse annuity mortgage (RAM)   A mortgage in which the borrower is paid an annuity (income) drawn against the equity in the home.

Right of survivorship   Right to acquire the interest of a deceased joint owner. Distinguishing characteristic of joint tenancy.

Right of way   A privilege given by the owner of a property to another, giving the right to pass over private land.

Riparian rights   The right of a landowner to water on, under, or adjacent to the land owned.

Sale-leaseback   A sale of a subsequent lease from the buyer back to the seller.

Savings and Loan Association   An institution that retains deposits for savers and lends out these deposits for home loans.

Secondary financing   A junior loan, second in priority to a first mortgage or trust deed.

Security deposit   Money given to a landlord by the tenant to secure performance of the rental agreement.

Sellers' market   A time when there are more buyers than sellers.

Severalty   An estate held by one person alone, an individual right. The term is misleading as it does not mean several persons own it. Distinguished from joint tenancy.

Shared appreciation   See equity sharing.

Shared appreciation mortgage (SAM)   A mortgage that allows the lender to share in the appreciation of the property in return for a lower rate of interest.

Sheriff's deed   Deed given by court order in connection with the sale of a property to satisfy a judgment.

Single-family residence   A general term to distinguish a house from an apartment house, a condominium, or a planned-unit development.

Special assessment   Legal charge against real estate by public authority to pay the cost of public improvements (for example, sewers) by which the property benefits.

Speculator   One who buys property with the intent of selling it quickly at a profit.

Straight-line depreciation   Reducing value for tax purposes over an extended period of time by equal increments.

Straight note   A non-amortized note promising to repay a loan, signed by the debtor and including the amount, date due, and interest rate.

Subdivision   A division of one parcel of land into smaller lots.

Subject-to mortgage   When a buyer takes title to real property "subject-to mortgage," buyer is not responsible to the holder of the note. The original maker of the note is not released from the liability of the note and the most the new buyer can lose in foreclosure is equity in the property.

Sublease   A lease given by a lessee.

Syndicate   A group of investors who invest in one or more properties through a partnership, corporation, or trust.

Take-out commitment   Agreement by a lender to have available a long-term loan over a specified time once construction is completed.

Tax base   The assessed value multiplied by the tax rate to determine the amount of tax due.

Tax sale   A sale of property, usually at auction, for nonpayment of taxes assessed against it.

Tenancy in common   Ownership by two or more persons who hold an undivided interest without right of survivorship.

Tenant   The holder of real property under a rental agreement. Also referred to as a lessee.

Tender   An offer of money, usually in satisfaction of a claim or demand.

Tenements   All rights in land which pass with the conveyance of the land. Also commonly refers to certain groups of multiple dwellings.

Testator   A person who leaves a legally valid will at death.

Tight money   A condition in the money market in which demand for the use of money exceeds the available supply.

Time-share   Shared ownership wherein the owners are allowed limited use of a property.

Title insurance   Insurance written by a title company to protect the property owner against loss if title is imperfect.

Topography   Character of the surface of land. Topography may be level, rolling or mountainous.

Township   A territorial subdivision six miles long, six miles wide, and containing 36 sections, each one mile square.

Tract house   A house similar to other homes within a subdivision and built by the same developer, as opposed to a custom home built to owner specifications.

Trade fixtures   Personal property of a business that is attached to the property, but can be removed upon the sale of the property.

Trust deed   An instrument that conveys legal title of a property to a trustee to be held pending fulfillment of an obligation, usually the repayment of a loan to a beneficiary (lender).

Trustee   One who holds bare legal title to a property in trust for another to secure performance of a debt obligation.

Trustor   The borrower of money secured by a trust deed.

Unimproved land   Land in its natural state without structures on it.

Unlawful detainer   An action of law to evict a person or persons illegally occupying real property.

Usury   Interest rate charged on a loan in excess of that permitted by law.

Variable-interest rate   A fluctuating interest rate that can go up or down depending on the market rate.

Vendee   A purchaser or buyer.

Vendor   A seller.

Vested   Bestowed upon someone or secured by someone, such as title to property.

Voluntary lien   A lien voluntarily put on by the owner, such as a mortgage, as opposed to an involuntary lien (for example, taxes).

Waive   To relinquish, or abandon. To forgo a right to enforce or require anything.

Wrap-around mortgage   A second mortgage that is subordinate to but includes the face value of the first mortgage. Also referred to as an All-Inclusive Trust Deed or AITD.

Yield   Ratio, expressed as a percentage, of income from an investment to the total cost of the investment over a given period of time.

Zoning   Act of city or county authorities specifying how property may be used in specific areas.

INDEX